Henry Stanley (left) and David Livingstone

THE WORLD'S GREAT EXPLORERS

Henry Stanley and David Livingstone

By Susan Clinton

Consultant: Laurence D. Schiller, Ph.D.,
Lecturer, Department of History,
Northwestern University, Evanston, Illinois

CHILDRENS PRESS ®

CHICAGO

David Livingstone in Africa

Opposite page:
Henry Stanley making his way through the African jungle

Editor: Ann Heinrichs
Designer: Linda anne Donohoe
Cover Art: Steven Gaston Dobson
Engraver: Liberty Photoengraving

**Library of Congress
Cataloging-in-Publication Data**

Clinton, Susan.
  Henry Stanley and David Livingstone / by
Susan Clinton.
    p.   cm. — (The World's great explorers)
  Includes bibliographical references and index.
  Summary: Describes the travels of Stanley
and Livingstone as they unlocked many
geographic secrets of Africa.
  ISBN 0-516-03055-8
  l. Livingstone, David, 1813-1873—Juvenile
literature. 2. Stanley, Henry M. (Henry
Morton), 1841-1904--Juvenile literature. 3.
Explorers—Africa, Sub-Saharan—Biography—
Juvenile literature. 4. Explorers—Great
Britain—Biography—Juvenile literature. 5.
Africa, Sub-Saharan—Discovery and explora-
tion—Juvenile literature. [1. Stanley, Henry
M. (Henry Morton), 1841-1904. 2. Livingstone,
David, 1813-1873. 3. Explorers.] I. Title. II.
Series.
DT1110.L58C55 1990
916.704'312'0922—dc20
[B]   90-2172
[920]   CIP

Table of Contents

Chapter 1
Dr. Livingstone, I Presume?

For once in his life, Henry Morton Stanley wasn't sure what to say. Stanley made his living by putting events into words—exciting, stirring words. He was a newspaperman; not the sort who sits behind a desk in an office, but a brash, roving reporter with a strong will, a quick wit, and a hot temper. These qualities didn't make him easy to get along with, but they made him a great reporter. Now, in November 1871, after walking more than 1,000 miles (1,609 kilometers) through east-central Africa, Stanley was about to walk into the news story of a lifetime. He had risked his life and spent thousands of dollars searching for the English explorer and missionary Dr. David Livingstone. Not until he was moments away from meeting Livingstone did Stanley realize with a jolt that he had no idea what to say to him.

Stanley had been preparing for this moment ever since he got the assignment. He was a reporter for the *New York Herald*, a newspaper that was well known and widely read, but hardly well respected. The owner of the *Herald*, James Gordon Bennett, wanted to keep his readers on the edge of their chairs. He wanted to get the news first, and it had better be sensational.

Bennett had a hunch that finding David Livingstone would be sensational. Livingstone had spent much of his life as a missionary and explorer in Africa. He wanted to open Africa to European Christianity and European trade. In order to do that, Livingstone kept searching for a waterway that would carry traders and missionaries into central Africa. Livingstone never succeeded in this search, although the discoveries he made along the way made him a national hero back in England. In 1849, he had been the first European to cross the Kalahari Desert and see Lake Ngami. In 1851, he was the first to see the world's greatest waterfall, which he named Victoria Falls after England's queen. In 1853–1856, he became the first to cross Africa, coast to coast.

In 1866, Livingstone went off on another African expedition. He planned to attack two problems that had been bothering him. First, Livingstone believed he could solve the great geographical mystery of his century: the source of the Nile River. He believed the source was a huge central African river, the Lualaba, but no one had ever traced its course. Livingstone was nearly sure that it emptied into the Nile, and he meant to prove this single-handedly.

The other problem weighing on his mind and conscience was the East African slave trade. The Arabs of East Africa had long been shipping African slaves to

James Gordon Bennett

A British ship attempting to stop a vessel engaged in the slave trade

Middle Eastern countries. In 1840, the Arab sultan of Oman established his rule on Zanzibar, an island off the East African coast. He gradually brought the coastal slave traders under his control and made Zanzibar the central marketplace for the East African slave trade. Every year, traders ventured deeper and deeper into Africa's interior to buy or capture thousands of men, women, and children for the slave markets of Zanzibar.

Livingstone hated the slave trade and all the cruelty and misery that went along with it. Since 1808, British ships had patrolled the West African coast searching suspicious-looking ships and freeing any slaves they found on board. Livingstone hoped that, by writing about the horrors of East African slaving, he could prompt his government to end the slave trade on the east coast, too.

The tasks Livingstone set for himself were huge; the territory he planned to cover was enormous. Livingstone had always liked to work "beyond every other man's line of things." Though there were some trails where he planned to travel, there were no paved roads, no newspapers, no maps, and no telegraph offices. His only companions on this ambitious and dangerous trip were hired carriers. Livingstone did not travel well with his own countrymen. With other Europeans, whether missionaries or fellow explorers, he was demanding, resentful, and stubborn. On the other hand, Livingstone generally got along well with Africans. In spite of the narrowness of his upbringing and his religious training, he was fascinated by African ways of life. He tried to understand African cultures instead of simply scorning them as primitive or savage. He filled his journals with information about the language and dress, farming techniques, and crafts of the Africans he met.

Serving in Zanzibar as British Consul for Inner Africa had been his last contact with western civilization. Once he headed inland in March 1866, Livingstone had to rely on Arab slave traders to carry his letters back to Zanzibar. Naturally, the slave traders did not want to carry letters back that condemned their way of life. Even when the Arabs were willing to help him, it was a slow and uncertain way to send a letter.

Many of Livingstone's letters never reached the coast. One letter that did get to the English consul arrived a full year after Livingstone wrote it. Isolated in the interior, Livingstone could only hope that news of his travels and discoveries would reach England. If he became seriously ill or ran out of supplies, he would

The pelele, or lip ring, used by some African peoples

A portion of Zanzibar's seacoast

have to trust this slow and unreliable line of communication for help.

When Livingstone left Zanzibar in 1866, he was fifty-three years old and his health was not good. Three years later, no one knew where he was or if he was even alive. Twice, British newspapers had printed news of his death. About this time, Bennett thought it was time to go out after him. So he called in his star reporter, Henry Stanley, and ordered him, "Find Livingstone."

Stanley knew that an expedition to search central Africa would be long and very expensive. When he asked Bennett about the cost, he answered, "Well, I will tell you what you will do. Draw a thousand pounds now; and when you have gone through that draw another thousand, and when that is spent, draw another thousand, and when you have finished that draw another thousand, and so on; but find Livingstone." (At that time, 1,000 British pounds would have been worth about 5,000 American dollars.)

Even with unlimited funds, the search for Livingstone would not be easy. But Stanley refused to be daunted. Once he arrived in Zanzibar, he bought 6 tons (5.4 metric tons) of supplies and hired two hundred porters to carry them. These huge purchases caused quite a stir among the Zanzibar merchants, but Stanley kept the purpose of his trip a secret. He didn't want anyone else to find the doctor before he did.

With no new information on Livingstone, Stanley would have to track him by instinct and hearsay. Most people in the African interior never saw white people. Stanley knew that they would remember a visit by Livingstone. And he had a rumor to go on—a white man had been seen in Ujiji two years earlier. Ujiji was an Arab trading post 800 miles (1,287 kilometers) inland on the shore of Lake Tanganyika.

Ujiji seemed like the best place to start looking, although getting there was much harder than Stanley had expected. Stanley had hired two Englishmen to help him manage the porters, but they died early in the trip. Stanley himself was very sick with malaria. This tropical disease first causes severe chills, then high fever, and finally, a period of heavy sweating. Once the sweating ends, it seems as if the disease is over, but in a day or two the whole cycle starts over again. As Stanley wrote, "Days of illness from fever had alternated with days of apparent good health."

A war between Arab traders and a powerful African chief held Stanley up for three months. Finally he decided to make a big detour to the south to avoid the fighting. This detour added several hundred miles to the trip and brought his caravan through country where food was scarce. All the trade goods Stanley had brought would be useless if the chiefs had no food to give. Nevertheless, Stanley felt he could wait no longer. Many of his porters had deserted. Some had been killed in the fighting. On their trek through the famine-stricken country, those carriers that were left came close to rebelling and killing Stanley.

Finally, after eight months of difficult travel, Stanley caught his first sight of Ujiji. He stopped outside the town to prepare for as grand an entrance as he could muster. He changed into clean white clothes and made all his carriers put on their best. All the men who carried muskets aimed at the sky and fired over and over again for the whole last mile into town. A crowd of Arabs and Africans quickly gathered to welcome the new arrivals, but Stanley kept looking for a white face. As Stanley and his followers neared the center of town, he saw a tall, worn-looking white man coming toward him.

At this moment of triumph, Stanley was suddenly uncertain. What should he say? What if it wasn't Livingstone? What if it was Livingstone and he was angry at being "found"? Later Stanley wrote about this moment: "All around me was the immense crowd, hushed and expectant, and wondering how the scene would develop itself."

Lake Tanganyika at Ujiji

Stanley and Livingstone meet in Ujiji in November 1871

Stanley was already thinking of this meeting as a scene, a scene in the story he would write for the *Herald*. Perhaps that is why he felt so suddenly unsure. Stanley knew he would make this scene go down in history, and he felt the pressure of future readers. Whatever he said, Stanley felt it should have some dignity. Finally, in a trembling voice, he said, "Dr. Livingstone, I presume?"

This stiff, formal greeting would seem funny to those thousands of readers, but Dr. Livingstone didn't laugh. Instead, the older man's eyes filled with tears as he shook hands with Stanley. It was indeed Dr. Livingstone. Far from feeling angry for being found, Livingstone was overwhelmed with gratitude.

Of course, Livingstone had never considered himself lost. But he did feel as if he had been forgotten by

everyone back home. Now here was Henry Stanley bringing news and letters and supplies. Livingstone was stunned by Stanley's supplies. He wrote of them in his journal: "Bales of goods, baths of tin, huge kettles, cooking pots, tents, &c., made me think 'This must be a luxurious traveller, and not one at his wits' end like me.'"

Dr. Livingstone's house at Ujiji

Just a month before Stanley arrived, Livingstone had struggled back to Ujiji to find himself stranded there. After six years in Africa, Livingstone's funds were exhausted. He had no money to pay carriers or to buy supplies. All Livingstone had left was a few yards of cloth that he could trade for some coarse grain and vegetables. But by now, his health was so bad that he could hardly digest the foods he could afford.

His medicines had all been lost when the man carrying them deserted the expedition in the middle of the thick jungle. The supplies he expected to find waiting for him in Ujiji had been sold off by the caravan leader who brought them in from Zanzibar. Until Stanley arrived, the explorer's only hope had been to hold out for ten months until fresh supplies could come in from Zanzibar.

That first night, the two of them drank the bottle of champagne that Stanley had brought 1,000 miles (1,609 kilometers) into Africa, just for this meeting. As Livingstone talked about his travels and discoveries, Stanley's admiration for him and his elation over finding him grew. At the same time, he couldn't help noting how thin the doctor was and how worn and patched his clothes were. Stanley decided to bring Livingstone back to health. He began to cook the doctor's food himself, with his own hands. Under the influence of Stanley's cooking and his cheering company, Livingstone fattened up. He wrote, "Appetite returned, and instead of the spare, tasteless two meals a day, I ate four times daily, and in a week began to feel strong."

Both Stanley and Livingstone could be thorny, difficult personalities, but somehow they brought out the best in each other. Stanley ended up staying with Livingstone for four months. Together they explored the north end of Lake Tanganyika. On this trip, it was Livingstone who had to nurse Stanley through several bouts of malaria. Although he was in great pain, Stanley wrote, "I did not much regret its occurrence, since I became the recipient of the very tender and fatherly kindness of the good man whose companion I now find myself."

Stanley had grown up without having a father. When he found Livingstone, he found a man he could love, respect, and learn from—as if Livingstone were the father he never had. Livingstone, on the other hand, had three sons and two daughters who grew to adulthood. He had ignored them while they lived with him in Africa and never really got to know them all. Livingstone was able to share his work and his thoughts with Stanley in a way that he had never done with his own children.

When Stanley had to leave, he tried to talk Livingstone into coming back with him to regain his health. Livingstone refused; he did not want to go home without finding the source of the Nile. So Stanley left him half of his supplies, including a tent, a boat, a bathtub, tools, medicine, paper, rifles, books, and new clothes. He promised to hire carriers for Livingstone and send them in from the coast. Stanley equipped Livingstone to go on and follow the Lualaba River, even though he had a feeling he would never see Livingstone alive again.

Livingstone's greatest comfort, however, was that he could trust Stanley to carry his letters and his journal back to England. Stanley took charge of the journal with the full sense of its value to both Livingstone and himself. These writings would prove he had really found the doctor.

The world did not hear of Stanley's success until May 1872, six months after their meeting. When the news came, it electrified readers on both sides of the Atlantic. Bennett, Stanley's publisher, telegraphed his congratulations: "You are now as famous as Livingstone, having discovered the discoverer. Accept my thanks and the whole world's."

Stanley never did see Livingstone again. Livingstone died in Africa in 1873. He had not succeeded in tracing the Lualaba or finding the source of the Nile. He didn't live to realize that he had helped to close the Zanzibar slave market. For some time, the English government had been pressuring the sultan of Zanzibar to limit the slave trade, but without much success. When Stanley returned, he made sure that Livingstone's account of the brutal East African slave trade was widely read. This aroused the public's conscience and made the slave trade issue more urgent.

John Kirk, the British consul in Zanzibar, was authorized to threaten the Zanzibari sultan. If the sultan did not end the slave trade, English ships would surround Zanzibar and cut off all trade. On June 5, 1873, just five weeks after Livingstone's death, the sultan agreed to close down the slave market.

Stanley's story brought new interest in Livingstone's writings and in his concerns for Africa. Livingstone had also had a special impact on Stanley. Stanley tried to explain it: "Somehow these dreams perpetually haunt me. I seem to see through the dim, misty, warm, hazy atmosphere of Africa always the aged face of Livingstone, urging me on in his own kind, fatherly way."

After Livingstone's death, Stanley decided to finish the great explorer's work. In an amazing feat of will and endurance, he led an expedition across Africa, following the Lualaba River to where it emptied into the Atlantic Ocean. Livingstone had been wrong about the Lualaba; it did not flow into the Nile, but into the Congo River. Stanley mapped the river system of central Africa and settled the question of the Nile's source once and for all. The real source of the

Nile was Lake Victoria, as English explorer John Hanning Speke had claimed years before. Speke had never been able to prove his claim; Stanley sailed all the way around the lake to do so. By the time Stanley finished Livingstone's task, he was famous not only as a writer, but as a great African explorer in his own right.

Livingstone and Stanley had tremendous effects on the relationship between Europe and Africa. They led the way into the continent by breaking paths into the African interior. They also opened up Africa to people's minds by describing the land, its peoples, and their cultures. Over and over again, they pointed out opportunities for mining, farming, trade, and settlement in Africa.

A French statesman once congratulated Stanley, saying: "Not only, sir, have you opened up a new continent to our view, but you have given impulse to scientific and philanthropic enterprises which will have a material effect on the rest of the world. . . . What you have done has influenced governments—proverbially so difficult to be moved—and the impulse you have imparted to them will, I am convinced, go on growing year after year."

These remarks came true. When Livingstone first went to Africa in 1841, Europeans had barely touched the edges of the continent. Between the northern Mediterranean coast and the British Cape Colony on the southern tip of the continent, European settlements were few and largely limited to coastal trading towns. Much of the African interior was unknown and unmapped territory. By the time Stanley died in 1904, most of Africa had been carved up into European colonies.

Chapter 2
No Time for Childhood

Ten-year-old David Livingstone had to keep his eyes on the cotton threads moving around the spinning frame in front of him. If any of these threads started to split or fray, he had to crawl in and around the machinery and piece the fraying thread back together. David and his two brothers had the same job at the cotton mill; they were called piecers.

The owners kept it hot in the mill where he worked, as hot as a summer day. The heat was supposed to be good for the thread, but it made it hard for David and the other children to keep awake, especially toward the end of the day. Workdays at the mills were long; men, women, and children started at six in the morning and didn't finish until eight at night. If any of the children dozed off, supervisors woke them harshly, either by dousing them with buckets of cold water or beating them with leather straps. Very few of these mill children would ever learn to read or write. Most of them were too tired to play. But even though he worked at the mill until he was twenty-three years old, David Livingstone did not wear out or give up.

David Livingstone was born on March 19, 1813, in Blantyre, Scotland. This little town, just eight miles (thirteen kilometers) outside of Glasgow, centered around the Blantyre cotton mill where David and his brothers worked. David's father, Neil, had grown up in Blantyre and worked in the mill as a boy. David's grandfather, also named Neil, had started out as a tenant farmer; that is, he rented the land that he farmed. When the landowner decided to get rid of the tenant farmers and raise sheep on the land instead, David's grandfather moved his family to Blantyre and took a job in the mill.

Factory work was a new way of life in 1792, when Neil Livingstone came to Blantyre. All over Scotland and England, thousands of families swarmed the cities and mill towns looking for some way to feed their families. People were used to living on the land, grow-

The room where David Livingstone was born, March 19, 1813

ing their own food, and spinning their own thread on spinning wheels at home. They would make as much as their own families needed. But in factories like the Blantyre mill, the machines spun thread much faster than anyone working at home could have done. Everybody in the mill made only thread and yarn all day long. Instead of growing the food they ate, workers now used their pay to buy food.

Unfortunately, the mill owners didn't pay the workers much money. So many people needed jobs that the owners could easily replace anyone who caused trouble. Factory work was still a new way of life in the early 1800s when David Livingstone was a boy. There were very few laws to protect workers. There were no laws against child labor and no laws limiting workdays to eight hours. Neither were there laws to protect workers who got hurt in the mill machinery or for piecers who grew up with crooked spines and bowed legs because of their work.

The owner of Blantyre mill did build housing for his workers. In these apartment buildings, each family had a room that measured ten by fourteen feet (three by four meters). Each had a fireplace for cooking and warmth and two alcoves for beds. David lived in one of these rooms with his parents and his four brothers and sisters.

The law did require factory owners to provide an education for their child workers. This the Blantyre owners did. Their company school was free to any child who had enough energy to go and study from eight to ten at night. David had the energy, and he was determined not to spend his life laboring at the mills. His father put a high value on education; he had already taught David to read and write at home.

The house where Livingstone lived during his youth

In school, David studied Latin. During work, he propped his Latin grammar up on the machinery. Then he studied it phrase by phrase as he moved back and forth piecing threads.

David had to be determined—he had to be stubborn—about getting an education; and he had to be willing to do it alone. At thirteen, he was the only student in a special Latin class. His fellow workers did not admire his determination; they made fun of him. Some of them made a game of throwing things to knock his books down, but ridicule did not stop David Livingstone. He could already think for himself.

David inherited his strong-minded independence from his father. As he grew up, he had to defend his interest in science against his father. David liked to spend what free time he had roaming the countryside collecting plants and rocks, which he would later identify. He read every science book he could get his hands on. Neil Livingstone didn't approve; he wanted to see David reading religious writings, not books about rocks and plants.

Neil Livingstone worked as a traveling tea salesman, although this job didn't bring in much money. Nonetheless, Neil Livingstone liked his job. Traveling and talking with people gave him a chance to carry out work he believed was much more important than selling tea or making money—spreading his religious beliefs.

It was finally one of his father's religious pamphlets that showed David how to combine his religious faith with his love of science. The pamphlet was all about the need for a new kind of missionary— missionary doctors who could cure illness as well as convert souls. As soon as he read it, David Livingstone knew the job was for him.

First, he would have to go through medical school. After saving his earnings for a year and a half, David had enough to start at Anderson College in Glasgow. One snowy day in 1836, he and his father walked the eight miles (thirteen kilometers) to the city. There they rented David a tiny room on a street named Rotten Row.

During the week, he went to lectures and watched doctors demonstrate their methods. In the 1830s, medicine was crude at best. No one understood that germs cause disease. Many believed that disease was caused by too much blood or by impurities in the blood. Their remedy was often to bleed the patient, that is, to cut a vein and let the patient lose some blood. Sometimes they put little blood-sucking worms called leeches on the patient's body.

Of course, the bleeding didn't cure the patients. In fact, it only made them weaker, but doctors didn't have a better way of treating illnesses. They did not yet have any drugs to dull pain, so operations had to be done as quickly as possible while the patient was awake. Tropical diseases like malaria, which Livingstone would suffer from again and again in Africa, were totally unknown in Europe.

When Livingstone had learned all he could at Anderson College, he applied to the London Missionary Society and was accepted. The society trained people to be preachers and sent them to teach Christianity in faraway countries. Missionaries were eager to spread their faith to the millions of people who knew nothing about the Christian God. They believed that people could only understand the meaning and value of their lives if they believed that Jesus Christ died for mankind. Missionaries were confident that Christianity would bring people new joy and dignity, thus improving their lives.

Most missionaries also believed that their Christian European way of life was better than any non-Christian customs or beliefs. This is probably why Livingstone's missionary training didn't teach anything about African people and cultures or about the dangers he might face. Instead, he learned to read the Bible in Hebrew and Greek and to argue the fine points of religious belief.

By the end of his training, Livingstone knew where he wanted to go. He didn't want an easy, settled post, where converts had already been made and churches built. He wanted to go where the need for both missionaries and doctors was greatest. He chose southern Africa. In 1840, he met Robert Moffat, one of the society's most successful missionaries. Moffat had spent nearly twenty years working in the southern African village of Kuruman. He told Livingstone about seeing "the smoke of a thousand villages where no missionary had ever been." This was exactly what Livingstone was after.

That same year, Livingstone was licensed as a doctor and ordained as a minister. On December 8, 1840, he boarded a sailing ship called the *George* for a three-month voyage to Cape Colony, a British settlement in southern Africa. The trip was no pleasure. Passengers were crowded in among their packing crates, and cockroaches swarmed over everything. In March 1841, Livingstone reached Cape Town, a small port at the southern tip of the African continent. After a few weeks' rest, Livingstone set out on the 600-mile (966-kilometer) trip north to Kuruman.

What would be a ten- or twelve-hour car trip today took Livingstone over two months by ox-wagon. It was winter, the dry season in southern Africa. The only greenery was, as Livingstone described it, "low stunted scraggy bushes, many of them armed with bent thorns villainously sharp and strong." The clumsy wagons rumbled along, with sacks of food slung down the sides and underneath them. Packing boxes were stacked high in the middle of each wagon; at night, travelers slept on top of the piles.

Despite all the difficulties, Livingstone immediately loved traveling in Africa. He had spent his childhood and young manhood working hard in narrow quarters. But here, the slow pace, the freedom to stop and camp wherever he liked, and the immense, empty landscape around him were all great pleasures to the young missionary on his way to a new life.

Chapter 3
No Place for a Child

In 1841, the same year that Livingstone first came to Africa, Henry Morton Stanley was born into a situation poorer and more miserable than Livingstone's had been. Stanley never liked to talk about his early life; he never celebrated his own birthday. Henry Stanley wasn't his real name. He was born John Rowlands on January 28, 1841, in Denbigh, Wales. His mother, Elizabeth Parry, wasn't married. She named her baby after a farmer who admitted he was the baby's father. But neither the father nor his family would have anything to do with this unwanted child. Soon after his birth, John's mother went to work as a servant, leaving her infant son behind.

For a few years, the little boy lived with his grandfather and his uncles. After his grandfather's death, however, his uncles were no longer willing to pay for his upkeep. On February 10, 1847, the frightened six-year-old was taken to the St. Asaph Union Workhouse, where he would live for the next nine years.

The purpose of the workhouse was to take care of those who couldn't take care of themselves: orphaned and deserted children, lunatics, the elderly poor, vagrants—all of society's outcasts. Public charity forbade letting these people starve to death, but it didn't go so far as to provide them with any comforts. In fact, the workhouse was run like a prison where the inmates were punished for their poverty and misfortune. Children and adults wore plain uniforms, ate meager meals of mostly bread and gruel, worked at house and garden chores most of the day, and were locked in their dormitories by eight o'clock at night.

According to Stanley, the worst thing about it was the schoolmaster, James Francis, who brutally slapped, kicked, and caned the thirty young boys in his care. The children lived in a constant state of fear of their teacher's violent outbursts. Stanley claimed that he himself ran away from the workhouse at the age of fifteen after a violent quarrel with Francis.

Once free, young John Rowlands made the rounds of his Welsh relatives, searching for someone to take him in. Several of his uncles fed him a meal and sent him away. Next, he visited his father's well-to-do father. Grandfather Rowlands told the thin young boy standing there in his workhouse uniform, "You can go back the same way you came. I can do nothing for you and have nothing to give you." Finally, he was grudgingly taken in, first by a schoolmaster cousin and then by a poor uncle in the port city of Liverpool, England. But he knew he wasn't welcome to stay anywhere for long. Wherever he went, John Rowlands had to depend on people who resented having to feed and shelter him. To feed his own family, the uncle in Liverpool even sold the clothes John had received from his cousin.

In his relatives' homes, John Rowlands was still an outcast.

All the grim city of Liverpool could offer was a life of poverty and humiliation. Rowlands made a bold decision. He signed on as a cabin boy on a ship bound for New Orleans. At seventeen, he had nothing to lose. During the seven-week voyage, the mates on the ship purposely mistreated Rowlands and other crew members. They wanted to make the lads desert the ship in New Orleans and thereby lose all their pay. Their strategy worked. In the bustling port of New Orleans, John Rowlands crept off the ship and hid on the docks in some bales of cotton. The next day, he went looking for a job. To his surprise, he found more than a job.

John approached a well-dressed man in front of a warehouse and asked, "Do you want a boy, sir?" The man was an Englishman named Henry Stanley. Stanley was a prosperous cotton broker. He traveled between cotton plantations up the Mississippi River and cotton wholesalers in New Orleans. Although he had always wanted children, Stanley had none of his own. Maybe it was Rowlands's question, or maybe it was his British accent, but Henry Stanley took an immediate interest in this boy. He took him to breakfast, then to a barber, and then helped him to land a clerical job at a warehouse.

Rowlands did very well at his job. In the workhouse and on shipboard, he had always had to be hardworking, respectful, and quick. Here, too, he was hardworking and eager to please. The difference here was that his employers appreciated his hard work and paid him for it. He received a salary of twenty-five dollars a month, enough to pay for his room and board and buy some clothes and books, too.

Little by little, John Rowlands realized that he had escaped his past. For the first time in his life, he was free of harsh authority, daily humiliation, and poverty. It was a thrilling feeling; he wrote, "Throughout America, my treatment from men would solely depend upon my individual character, without regard of family or pedigree. These were proud thoughts . . . my shoulders rose considerably, my back straightened, my strides became longer, as my mind comprehended this new feeling of independence."

Henry Stanley, the cotton broker, continued to befriend Rowlands. He invited him to Sunday dinner, showed him the city, gave him books, and generally helped him learn how to behave in society. It was Stanley who bought Rowlands his first toothbrush and taught him how to use it. He got this silent, unemotional boy to open up and talk. Finally, the older man told John Rowlands to think of himself as a son. As a sign of their new relationship, John Rowlands changed his name to Henry Stanley. When the older Stanley hugged him, the young man burst into tears. In his autobiography he wrote, "It was the only tender action I had ever known."

The elder Stanley spent the next nine months traveling with his adopted son until some serious quarrel arose between them. Stanley never revealed what they fought about. But his stepfather placed Stanley with an Arkansas merchant and then went on to Cuba on business. The two men never saw one another again, although the young man kept the name Henry Stanley the rest of his life. He even wrote to a relative in Wales that John Rowlands was dead.

In Arkansas, Stanley got to know the touchy Southern planters who were always ready to pull out their

Capture of a Confederate battery during the Battle of Shiloh in the American Civil War

guns to settle a quarrel or avenge an insult. Stanley himself learned to shoot there, practicing until he "could sever a pack-thread at twenty paces." It was no surprise to the Arkansas planters when their state joined the Confederacy and entered the Civil War in 1861. It did surprise Stanley, who had paid no attention to American politics. He didn't want to get involved in this American fight. But when someone mailed him a woman's petticoat, he volunteered to fight rather than sit home and be branded a coward.

Stanley's Confederate regiment did its first fighting at the Battle of Shiloh, which began on April 6, 1862. On the second day of battle, Stanley ran out into an open space and threw himself into a hollow. When he looked around, he found himself surrounded by blue uniforms; he had run too far ahead. The Union soldiers took him prisoner.

Ten days later, Stanley found himself in a prisoner-of-war camp in Chicago, Illinois. Hundreds of men were penned in a muddy yard with a row of long barracks buildings. For a bathroom, there was an open ditch behind the barracks. Sickness spread quickly through the crowded, dirty camp. Every day dead bodies were piled into wagons. A camp official offered Stanley a way out: he could join the Union army. At first Stanley refused, but six weeks later he was willing to change sides just to get out of the deadly camp. After two days in a blue uniform, Stanley became ill with dysentery, which he probably caught in prison. He was so sick that the Union army discharged him.

For the next few years Henry Stanley traveled about, supporting himself in whatever way he could. He worked on merchant ships and in a legal office. He volunteered for the navy, became a ship's clerk, and deserted seven months later. Next, he headed West to prospect for gold in Colorado. On the way back, he arranged to write articles about life out West for a St. Louis newspaper, the *Missouri Democrat*. In July 1866, Stanley set out to cross Asia, but he and his companions didn't get very far. Early in the trip they were captured, beaten, and robbed of everything they had.

Rescued with the help of an American minister, Stanley next had a naval officer's uniform made up for himself and wore it home to Wales to impress his relatives. In December 1866, he even went back to St. Asaph Workhouse. There he feasted the boys on tea and cakes and encouraged them all to work hard so that they could make a success of their lives as he had. Of course, all the while he was posing as a naval officer, Stanley knew that he still had no real place in

Henry Stanley at age nineteen

the world, no home, no job, no clear goals. He was so hungry for admiration and acceptance that he was willing to win it utterly on false grounds.

Twenty-two-year-old Henry Stanley

Back in St. Louis in February 1867, Stanley got the *Democrat* to pay him fifteen dollars a week to follow and report on the efforts of a peace commission to make treaties with the Indians. Stanley did a good job. He had an article in the paper almost every day. He covered the treaty dealings and threw in lots of colorful description on the side. While he wrote for the *Democrat*, Stanley also sent articles to papers in Chicago and New York. When the peace commission finished its work, Stanley was once more out of a job. He went to New York, walked into the *New York Herald* offices, and proposed to the owner, James Gordon Bennett, Jr., that he hire Stanley to cover a war in Abyssinia.

Abyssinia was the name of an area in present-day Ethiopia. Theodore, its king, had become a mad tyrant. Grieved over an insult, he was holding the British consul and about twenty missionaries in jail. The British were going to land a huge invading force and attack Theodore in his fortress capital, Magdala.

Bennett didn't think Americans were very interested in Abyssinia. But if Stanley would pay his own way, Bennett agreed that the *Herald* would buy the articles he sent back. Stanley accepted and left for Abyssinia two days later on December 22, 1867. On his way to catch up with the British army, Stanley made sure to visit the telegraph office in Suez, Egypt. All news from Magdala would have to travel through this office. To make sure that his stories would get out first, Stanley shrewdly paid the head telegraph operator a large bribe.

Henry Morton Stanley in 1867

As it turned out, the British conquered Magdala with very little fighting. Now Stanley had to beat the British reporters back to Suez to file his story. He rode ahead of them, swimming his horse across a swollen river, and caught a ship up the Red Sea coast to Suez. The telegraph office, as promised, sent Stanley's story on to the *Herald* well before any of the other reporters' stories. The British government had to read the *Herald* to find out what happened to their own army. This irritated the British government and all the other papers; however, it pleased James Gordon Bennett immensely. He offered Stanley a job as roving correspondent, with the splendid salary of 400 British pounds (2,000 American dollars) per year.

Bennett was a demanding employer; he kept Stanley traveling all over the world. In 1868, Stanley heard a rumor that Dr. Livingstone was coming home from Africa. Stanley rushed to Aden, in Arabia, to wait for more news about the famous explorer. He waited there ten weeks, but there was no further word of Livingstone. In October 1869, Bennett gave Stanley a list of assignments. He was to go to the opening of the Suez Canal, visit Jerusalem, travel across Iran and view the ancient ruins, and wind up in India. If Livingstone was still lost, his next job was to march into Africa and find him. Stanley had won the assignment that would change his life.

David Livingstone in his days as an earnest missionary

Chapter 4
God's Highway

The meeting between Stanley and Livingstone was still thirty years in the future when David Livingstone arrived at Kuruman on July 31, 1841. He expected to see a bustling Christian community. After all, Kuruman had been held up as a model mission post, the missionary society's greatest success in Africa. Robert Moffat had devoted twenty years to converting the people at Kuruman.

What he saw was a tiny village isolated in the middle of the desert. Although three hundred fifty people attended church services, only forty of them were full converts. Many probably came out of gratitude for the missionaries' help with mending guns and building irrigation ditches. Others may have come only out of politeness. Worse yet, the people there were cattle farmers who were likely to leave Kuruman and move their herds to better grazing land. Livingstone was bitterly disappointed. He began to realize that he himself was not willing to spend his life working in such isolation for such small results. He felt there must be a larger field for his efforts.

After only a month in Kuruman, Livingstone began making trips to the north, farther away from any European settlements. He was looking for a more populated place where he could make a fresh start. First he and another missionary named Roger Edwards got permission from a chief to come and live among the Bakhatla people in a place called Mabotsa, about 250 miles (402 kilometers) northeast of Kuruman. Livingstone went eagerly. He and Edwards began building huts, digging irrigation ditches, and preaching to the Bakhatla. Immediately Livingstone began to see why it was so hard to make converts.

The Bakhatla were fascinated to see white men. People watched everything Livingstone did; they wanted to touch his straight hair and his white face. They were astounded by his mirror and his watch. But these things also made many of them think Livingstone was a wizard who could curse them with a glance. Although the Bakhatla listened politely to his preaching, they couldn't take Livingstone's religion seriously. When he knelt down and bowed his head to pray, the Africans laughed at him. They thought he was praying to something that lived under the ground. As he learned the Bakhatla language, he realized that the word the missionaries were using for "holy" actually meant "a nice fat cow." The word they used for "sin" also meant "cow dung"; the closest he could come to saying "soul" was a word that meant "steam."

Mabotsa was in lion country. On February 16, 1844, Livingstone went to drive a lion away from a herd of sheep. He shot the lion but didn't kill him. Before Livingstone could reload, the enraged lion attacked, crushing Livingstone's shoulder and shaking his whole body "as a terrier dog does a rat." An African compan-

Livingstone attacked by the lion

ion shot at the lion and made it drop Livingstone.
Finally the lion dropped dead from its wounds. Since
Livingstone was the only doctor in Mabotsa, he had to
direct Edwards in setting his torn and fractured arm.
He lay helpless and in great pain in Edwards's hut for
weeks. For the rest of his life, Livingstone wouldn't be
able to lift his left arm higher than his shoulder.

The Africans' indifference to Christian teachings
worried Livingstone more than the lions did. He decided to leave and look for a more receptive group.

On January 2, 1845, Livingstone married Mary
Moffat, daughter of Robert Moffat. It was a practical
marriage. Mary was used to the hardships of Africa,
she was devoted to Livingstone, and he needed a wife.
He described her in a letter: "Mine is a matter of fact
lady, a little thick black haired girl, sturdy and all I
want." Starting a mission wouldn't be so lonely now.

Livingstone next went to the Bakwena, another group of southern African peoples. He settled at a place called Chonuane until the water supply dried up, and then moved with the Bakwena to a new settlement called Kolobeng. Here Livingstone made his first and only convert, the Bakwena chief, Sechele. This was a spectacular conversion. But the rest of the Bakwena, instead of following their chief's lead, were very distressed at his change of heart. After Livingstone persuaded Sechele to stop casting spells to bring rain, his people blamed Livingstone for the drought. Then, to conform to Christian teachings, Sechele decided to get rid of all but one of his wives. This alarmed the Bakwena severely. The chief's power was based on marriage alliances with many powerful families. Sending back these wives was politically dangerous for Sechele and upsetting for the whole group. The day of Sechele's baptism was a day of mourning for the Bakwena.

Livingstone was beginning to understand that the principles of Protestant Christianity went against all the values that held members of a clan together. African clans thought about survival and happiness for their whole group. The idea that each person attained salvation separately made no sense to them. Once again, Livingstone began to feel that it was useless to hang on in the same settlement waiting for converts.

Once more Livingstone traveled north, looking for a group even more remote from European contact than the Bakwena. He was able to do his exploring with the help of a friend and traveling companion, William Charles Oswell. Oswell was a wealthy Englishman who enjoyed traveling and hunting. He pro-

Livingstone at Lake Ngami

vided money and supplies for their journeys, and he was willing to let Livingstone take credit for any discoveries. On an expedition in 1849, Oswell, Livingstone, and a third companion had been the first Europeans to see Lake Ngami, in present-day Botswana.

In order to reach Lake Ngami, they had driven oxwagons across the Kalahari Desert. Because of the brutal heat, the oxen could only travel in the early morning and late afternoon. In the desert haze, the Kalahari's great salt flats looked just like lakes. One of these mirages was so convincing that even the expedition's dogs and horses ran toward it, hoping for a drink.

Livingstone and Oswell had heard rumors of a country to the north, "a country full of rivers—so many no one can tell their number—and full of large trees." This excited Livingstone. Most Europeans believed that all of central Africa was an empty desert. Reaching this country would not only be a great geographical discovery, but it might prove to be the new mission field Livingstone was looking for. Moreover, if there were countless rivers, perhaps missionaries could reach this country easily by river, without laboring across the terrible Kalahari.

Now, in 1851, Livingstone and Oswell explored even farther north than they had before. Each day, the first task in making camp was to dig for water. Sometimes none could be found. Livingstone had brought along his pregnant wife and their three children, all under six years old. Once they had to walk five days in the heat without any water. By this time they had swollen lips and black tongues. David and Mary Livingstone were afraid their children were going to die before their eyes. Later, Livingstone tried to make light of this, writing, "The less there was of water, the more thirsty the little rogues became."

At last, after a 700-mile (1,127-kilometer) trek, they arrived in an area ruled by people called the Makololo. The Makololo welcomed Livingstone immediately and invited him to travel through their country. Livingstone and Oswell came to the banks of a great river, 500 yards (457 meters) across. It was the Zambezi, a river that flowed on for 1,000 miles (1,609 kilometers), from present-day Angola south through Zambia, then east along the border between Zambia and Zimbabwe, and finally through Mozambique to the East African coast. This river could be what Liv-

ingstone thought of as "God's Highway"—the highway that would bring traders and missionaries into the interior.

Cape Town and Table Mountain in southern Africa

Livingstone was determined to find out; he wanted to explore the routes to the coasts, east and west. However, he realized that he could neither take his family on such a journey nor leave them behind. The only solution was to send them back to England. Livingstone took his family south all the way to Cape Town and put them on a ship. He trusted the London Missionary Society to support them while he was opening up new territory for missionary work. As it turned out, the society was not generous to the Livingstones. Mary and the children would go through four years of poverty and loneliness in England, a country that didn't feel like home to any of them.

Although he missed his family, Livingstone had his mind set on the Makololo and the Zambezi. On his return, Livingstone realized why the Makololo chief, Sekeletu, was so eager to welcome white men. The presence of Europeans and their guns meant protection from enemies. Pushed out of southern Africa by warfare, the Makololo had come to settle in the swampy area between the Chobe and Zambezi rivers. The rivers protected them from attack by the Ndebele, another migrating group that settled to the south of the Makololo. The rivers offered great natural protection. To reach the Chobe River, one had to cross a wide belt of reeds six to eight feet (two to two-and-a-half meters) tall. Travelers would have to lean against the reeds and bend them down to move forward even a few feet. Once in a while, Livingstone was lucky and found a section of reeds that had been flattened by a hippopotamus.

While the Makololo were safe from any surprise attacks, they were plagued by malaria. No one yet understood that mosquitoes carried this disease. Malaria had not bothered them in the drier southern climate; Livingstone and the Africans believed it was the damp swamp air that brought on the fever. The Makololo would boil roots and make steam baths to try to cure the disease. Livingstone knew, at least, that quinine would help. But the disease was definitely thinning the tribe. Chief Sekeletu hoped that Livingstone would help the Makololo get guns to fight their way to healthier ground or that he would have some influence with the Ndebele. After all, Livingstone's father-in-law, the Kuruman missionary Robert Moffat, had worked among the Ndebele and become very friendly with their chief.

While staying with the Makololo, Livingstone himself caught malaria for the first time. In his five months at Linyanti, their major settlement, he had eight attacks. His tongue hurt, his face was covered with boils, and his stomach hurt so much it felt as if it would burst. He also suffered painful vomiting and diarrhea. He was sure it would not be safe for other missionaries to come to this swampy country.

When he was well enough, Livingstone wanted to start exploring the route to the west coast. He persuaded Sekeletu to assign him twenty-seven men for an expedition from Linyanti to the port of Luanda. Luanda is on the coast of present-day Angola; in Livingstone's time, Angola was a Portuguese colony.

Sekeletu sent along some ivory elephant tusks, which Livingstone was to trade for some wonderful European goods he had described to the chief. On November 11, 1853, Livingstone and his Makololo porters set out, paddling canoes up the Zambezi all day and camping on the riverbank every night. By the campfire, Livingstone described nature along the river. He wrote about a fish-hawk diving down to steal a fish out of a pelican's purse-like beak; about young hippos riding on their parents' backs; and about the strong, musky taste of alligator meat, "not at all inviting for anyone except the very hungry."

When the river narrowed, they began traveling on foot through dense forest. The rainy season began in January. Rain pelted down every day as Livingstone and his men hacked a trail through the tangle of vines and undergrowth. Livingstone's medical instruments rusted; his clothes and his tent mildewed. The ground where they slept was so drenched that they had to dig drainage ditches around their sleeping spots.

David Livingstone in his traveling clothes

On the early part of their journey, the people they met were friendly and generous with gifts of food. In the village of one chief named Shinte, they were given a grand, ceremonious welcome, complete with the music of drums and marimbas. In Shinte's village, Livingstone met two Portuguese traders who were busy building up a square pen for captured slaves. The Portuguese paid African groups, such as the nearby Maribari, to conduct raids and bring in the men, women, and children that they captured. Children were especially valuable because they would not remember their homes well enough to run away.

Chief Shinte offered Livingstone a ten-year-old girl slave as a gift. It was very difficult for Livingstone to explain why he didn't want this gift. "On thanking him, and saying that I thought it was wrong to take away children from their parents, that I wished him to give up this system altogether, and trade in cattle, ivory, and bee-wax . . . he thought I was dissatisfied and sent for one a head taller." Of course, Livingstone refused to accept a taller girl, too.

The closer Livingstone came to the coast, the more the tribes he met had been corrupted by the influence of the slave trade. Instead of giving food to travelers out of generosity, they demanded payment in advance. Chiefs also demanded *hongo*—payment for the privilege of passing through their territory. The slave traders paid *hongo* so that the chiefs would return any escaped slaves. As a result, Livingstone wrote, "The independent chiefs . . . became excessively proud and supercilious in their demands, and look upon white men with the greatest of contempt."

One group called the Chiboque surrounded Livingstone and his men, waving their spears and demand-

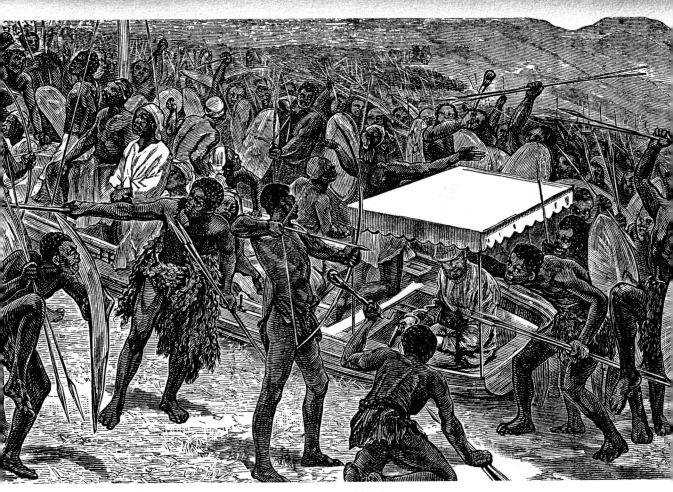

Livingstone surrounded by the Chiboque warriors

ing either a man, an ox, or a gun. Livingstone sat calmly in the center of the circle holding two loaded guns while the Makololo edged behind the Chiboque chiefs with their spears. After several gifts were rejected, Livingstone said, "it was evident that they wanted to fight, while we only wanted to pass peaceably through the country; that . . . we would not fight until they had struck the first blow. I then sat silent for some time. It was rather trying for me, because I knew that the Chiboque would aim for the white man first; but I was careful not to appear flurried, and having four barrels ready for instant action, looked quietly at the savage scene around." The Chiboque decided to settle for an ox.

Livingstone needed his oxen. When they couldn't afford to buy food from the chiefs, Livingstone's men would slaughter one of their own oxen for food. Livingstone was so weak from repeated malaria attacks that he needed to ride instead of walk. Malaria left him giddy, so that he fell off his ox several times a day. Sinbad, the ox he rode, also had an evil temper. He seemed to delight in running under low vines, knocking Livingstone off, and kicking him as he ran ahead. Livingstone wrote that he was so sick and weak that these falls and kicks rarely bothered him.

On the banks of a deep river, Livingstone was faced by a demand for a man before the chief would loan any canoes. They needed canoes; the river was deep and full of poisonous water snakes. Livingstone had three oxen left and no trade goods. His clothes were in tatters and he was so weak he could barely stand. He couldn't meet the chief's demands, and it looked as if there was no way out except to fight.

Unexpectedly, Livingstone was rescued by a Portuguese sergeant who helped them get canoes and feasted Livingstone and his men at his home across the river. They had arrived on the outskirts of the Portuguese colony of Angola. From here to the coast, they could march from one little settlement to another. The Portuguese made sure they had good guides and lots of food. Once at the sea, the Makololo gazed in awe. They told Livingstone, "We marched along with our father [Livingstone], believing that what the ancients had always told us was true, that the world has no end; but all at once the world said to us, 'I am finished; there is no more of me!'"

In the port town of Luanda, British ships in the harbor offered to take Livingstone back to England, but he refused. He had two reasons. One was that the Makololo would never make it back to Linyanti without his help. The second was that he had not found that highway to the interior he had been seeking. The dense forest, malarial swamps, and hostile tribes made the route too dangerous. He had to go back to Linyanti and search for a path to the east coast.

The Portuguese generously sent him off with plenty of cloth, ammunition, and beads. All his men received muskets and new clothes. By the time Livingstone and his men made it back to Linyanti in September 1855, they had used up all these goods in paying *hongo* and buying food. At least they could present Chief Sekeletu with a colonel's uniform, sent along by the merchants of Luanda.

The Makololo were delighted to see Livingstone and his men again, almost two years after they had left, even though they came back empty-handed. When Livingstone proposed another trip, this time to the east coast, Sekeletu readily provided 114 men, as well as oxen, beads, and some food.

Soon after starting out, Livingstone's men rowed him to a little island in the Zambezi, right on the lip of a tremendous waterfall. Livingstone crept to the edge of the island and saw water cascade down about 350 feet (107 meters) into a narrow chasm. The force of the waterfall was so great that the clouds of vapor rose 300 feet (91 meters) into the air. That is why the Africans called the falls Mosi-oa-tunya, "the smoke that thunders." Livingstone was the first European to see it; he renamed the waterfall, which is located between present-day Zimbabwe and Zambia, the Victoria Falls. The little island where he landed is now named after him.

Victoria Falls

The beauty of Victoria Falls didn't move Livingstone as much as the discovery of the Batoka Plateau, an area of high ground just north of the Zambezi in the southwestern part of present-day Zambia. The country here was beautiful and lush, yet it was elevated enough that there were no swamps, no malaria. Here was the place for a mission post.

The Batoka chief said he would welcome a missionary, but Livingstone did not have much respect for the Batoka. He did not find their customs appealing. For one thing, all the Batoka knocked out their two front teeth. To them, anyone who kept teeth looked ugly, "like a zebra." Their way of greeting strangers was to lie on the ground, roll back and forth, and slap their thighs while yelling *"kina bomba."* The Batoka had been conquered and reconquered by three different tribes, so when Livingstone promised that the white men would bring peace, the Batoka made him very welcome.

On this trip, Livingstone had learned not to travel in the heavy rains. When a downpour started, his men took shelter under makeshift grass huts, while he sat on a camp stool under his umbrella and kept perfectly dry. He didn't suffer from malaria on this trip, and a sense of well-being and happiness shows in his notes.

One day he saw all sorts of tiny insects crawling on the packing boxes, "one of green and gold preening its wings, which glanced in the sun with metallic luster; another clear as crystal; a third the color of vermillion; and a fourth black. . . . In the quietest parts of the forest there is heard a faint but distinct hum, which tells of insect joy. One may see many whisking about in the clear sunshine in patches among the green glancing leaves; but there are invisible myriads working with never-tiring mandibles on leaves, and stalks, and beneath the soil. They are all brimful of enjoyment."

Past the Batoka Plateau, Livingstone followed the Zambezi east towards the Portuguese colony of Mozambique. Just as before, the closer he got to the Portuguese colony, the more hostile and demanding the chiefs were. At one point, a chief named Mpende ordered that no white man was to cross the river. Mpende had been fighting with the Portuguese. But once he learned that Livingstone was not Portuguese but English, "one of that tribe that loves the black men," he became very friendly.

Mpende advised Livingstone to cross the river and go overland to Tete, a Portuguese settlement about 250 miles (402 kilometers) from the coast. This way, he would avoid a rocky and twisting part of the river. Livingstone took his advice. By doing so, he missed a very difficult part of the Zambezi called the Quebrabasa Rapids. If he had seen these rapids, he would have known that the Zambezi was impassable. No ship could get through the thirty miles (forty-eight kilometers) of rocky, uphill rapids. But Livingstone didn't see them. He proceeded into the Portuguese settlement and arrived at the coast, convinced that the Zambezi was the trade route he had been seeking.

Between September 1854 and May 1856, Livingstone had crossed Africa from coast to coast, from Luanda in the west to the port of Quelimane on the east coast. He was not the first to travel coast to coast;

Zambezi River near Victoria Falls

Farming in central Africa

two Arab traders had done it before him, as had two African traders. But he was the first European to make the crossing. Back in England, the Royal Geographical Society was waiting to celebrate his feat of exploration. A British ship had been waiting at Quelimane to take him home.

Livingstone was happy because he believed his trip had opened the African interior to trade and Christianity. He envisioned a stream of traders and missionaries sailing up the Zambezi to the Batoka Plateau. Just then, a letter from the London Missionary Society squashed his hopes. The society wrote that it could not afford "to venture upon untried, remote, and difficult fields of labour." They would not follow up on his discoveries. Livingstone sailed home determined to talk someone into trying his highway into the central African heartland.

Chapter 5
The Zambezi Fiasco

In England, Livingstone was a national hero. He turned his journal notes into a book entitled *Missionary Travels and Researches in South Africa*, which sold a whopping seventy thousand copies. People swarmed to hear his lectures, and they liked what they heard about the Batoka Plateau. As contributions began to stream in, the London Missionary Society gave in to Livingstone. In May 1856, they agreed to start two new missions: Livingstone would lead one to the Makololo, while Robert Moffat would move north from Kuruman to work with the Makololo's enemies, the Ndebele. Livingstone had explained how important it was that he and Moffat be there. Because of Moffat's friendship with the Ndebele chief, they could manage to keep peace between the tribes. Then Livingstone could persuade the Makololo to move to the more healthful Batoka Plateau.

Dr. Livingstone's steamboat for exploring the Zambezi River

The mission plans moved forward until October. Then Livingstone stunned the London Missionary Society by announcing that he had accepted an offer from the British government to lead an expedition up the Zambezi. Officially he would be a roving consul to central Africa, with five times the salary he earned as a missionary. Moreover, the government was putting up 5,000 pounds (25,000 American dollars) to build a steamship and send a team of professional assistants —an engineer, an artist, a naval officer, a botanist, and a geologist. Livingstone added his own brother, Charles, as a moral officer.

Their plan was to steam up the Zambezi River to the Batoka Plateau and there study growing conditions and mineral resources. They sailed from England in a ship called the *Pearl* on March 10, 1858, and reached the mouth of the Zambezi two months later. Here the expedition members learned what Livingstone had not fully explained in his glowing picture of God's Highway: the Zambezi was not a deep and clear-flowing river. It was shallow and broken by mud flats and sandbars.

Livingstone had hoped that the *Pearl* could carry them upstream to Tete, past the worst of the low, malarial swamps, but the river was too shallow for the *Pearl*. Instead the expedition members had to disembark, unload all their supplies, and assemble a small steamship they had brought along. The little ship was named the *Ma-Robert*. That was the Makololo name for Livingstone's wife—mother of Robert, the Livingstones' oldest son.

Livingstone had prepared everyone for a great adventure, but he had not dwelt on the sheer physical discomfort of working in 100-degree heat (38-degree

Celsius) in a cloud of mosquitoes. The *Ma-Robert* also burned more than two tons (1.8 metric tons) of wood for each day of steam power. The men paid Africans along the shore to cut wood while they spent hours every day pulling the ship over sandbars.

This was hard work for healthy men, but by now almost all of Livingstone's European assistants were sick with their first attacks of malaria. Livingstone had not warned them about this, either. In fact, although he had nearly died from malaria himself, Livingstone reported that the disease itself was no worse than the common cold. All the expedition accomplished in its first six months was to carry its own supplies up the river to Tete.

The next step was to explore the little section of the river that Livingstone had bypassed on his coast-to-coast trip back in 1856. In November, Livingstone led his expedition upriver toward the Quebrabasa Rapids. On the second day, the river had narrowed to thirty feet (nine meters) across, and it was hard for the ship to fight against the current. Instead of the low jungle banks, high black cliffs rose on both sides of the river. At the first rapids, the *Ma-Robert* bashed into a rock and got a hole in its side.

The men had to leave the boat and climb the riverbanks on foot. The riverbanks were not gentle slopes, but piles of smooth, black boulders. These rocks were slippery and burning hot—the thermometer showed temperatures as high as 130 degrees Fahrenheit (54 degrees Celsius). Several of the men were too weak from malaria to keep up. The porters' feet and hands were covered with blisters. After four days of climbing, Livingstone decided he had not seen anything that a powerful ship could not barrel its way through.

Just as they were turning back, one of the Makololo remembered hearing of a place so terrible that even a thirsty man would be afraid to approach it. Except for Livingstone and the botanist, John Kirk, all the men were too tired to go any farther. The two went on alone for two days until they came to a place where the water cascaded down thirty feet (nine meters). Kirk knew that no ship would make it up or down through these falls.

All Livingstone's plans, for the Zambezi River and for the Batoka Plateau, were now impossible. No missionaries or traders would be able to get past the Quebrabasa Rapids. But Livingstone did not admit that the rapids had ruined his dreams. In his letters he wrote, "I have not the smallest doubt but a steamer of good power could pass up easily in the flood." Then he asked the British government to send a more powerful steamer.

Meanwhile, Livingstone came up with a new goal for his expedition. Perhaps the Zambezi wasn't God's Highway after all. He chose a new river called the Shire, which flowed south through present-day Malawi into the Zambezi. He heard that the Shire flowed out of a great lake down through the high country. In his mind, this high country, the Shire Highlands, had already replaced the Batoka Plateau as the ideal spot for British settlement. On January 1, 1859, the *Ma-Robert* steamed up the Shire. Eight days upriver they ran into a thirty-mile (forty-eight kilometer) stretch of rapids. Livingstone named them the Murchison Falls after the president of the Royal Geographic Society. Once again, the ship could not go on and Livingstone and his companion, Kirk, had to hike along on foot.

About 200 miles (322 kilometers) north of

The discovery of Lake Nyasa

Murchison Falls, Livingstone and Kirk arrived on the shore of the second-largest lake in Africa, Lake Nyasa. This lake, now called Lake Malawi, is the source of the Shire River. The surrounding Shire Highlands were all he could hope for—beautiful, well-watered high country, perfect for British settlement, except for one terrible problem.

All along the Zambezi, the people they met had been friendly, curious, and willing to trade for food. All along the Shire, Livingstone noticed that the Manganja were very unfriendly. Either they ran away at the ship's approach, or they gathered on the shore to fire poison arrows. By the time he reached Lake Nyasa, Livingstone understood why. The Arabs were conducting regular slave raids up near the lake.

Livingstone freeing an enslaved African from captivity

In the countryside just south of Lake Nyasa, Livingstone and Kirk came across piles of taming sticks. These were large tree branches, forked on both ends. The forked branches would be laid on a slave's shoulders, and a metal bar fitted across the opening so that the slave could not pull his head out. One slave would be bolted into each end of the taming stick. So encumbered, they would not be able to run away. Besides, marching along carrying the heavy stick, and a load of ivory as well, would help to wear down any fighting spirit the captives had left. With the slave raids and the warfare between the Ajawa and the Manganja, the whole region was in upheaval.

Seeing this, Livingstone became so discouraged that he would sit for days, even weeks at a time, staring blankly into space. He wouldn't talk to anyone; he neither praised his assistants' efforts nor sympathized with their illness. Instead he seemed to expect that his European companions would show the same physical ruggedness and absolute dedication that he himself had. Yet, since he wouldn't tell them his plans, they had no idea what the expedition's goals now were. For men depending on his leadership, this was very alarming. The naval officer already had a dispute with Livingstone and left the expedition. Now Livingstone began to find fault with one after another of his assistants.

Livingstone fired the expedition geologist, Richard Thornton, for laziness in June 1859. At twenty-one, Thornton was the youngest member of the expedition. Livingstone had wanted him to dig out a thirty-foot (nine-meter) coal shaft to fuel the *Ma-Robert*. Thornton had trouble directing the Africans because he couldn't speak their language. Besides malaria, Thornton had painful boils on his feet and painful mosquito bites all over his legs that turned into sores. Still, he had gotten fifteen feet (4.6 meters) of the mine excavated. This wasn't enough for Livingstone. He dismissed Thornton, writing that he made "every allowance for your suffering from prickly heat and other little illnesses."

In 1860, Livingstone went back to the Makololo at Linyanti. Back in England, Livingstone had insisted that the London Missionary Society send missionaries to the Makololo, even though he himself wouldn't be with them. At his urging, the society had sent two missionaries there with their wives and children. Without Livingstone, their mission was doomed from the start. Chief Sekeletu had supported Livingstone's journeys because he expected both help against his enemies and a profitable trade with the coast. He had no use for these missionaries. Not only did the chief refuse to move his tribe out of the swampy land, he refused to let the missionaries move out either.

Within a few months, one of the missionaries, both of their wives, and three of their children had died miserably of malaria. The only survivors, Roger Price and his two children, had barely made it back to Cape Town.

When Livingstone learned of this disaster, he was immediately concerned—not for the suffering and loss the survivors had endured, but for his own reputation. He didn't want to be blamed for putting these missionaries into a hopeless situation, so he tried to turn the blame on them. He wrote angry letters back to England accusing Price of lying about the Makololo's hostility. He urged more missionaries to come out, even though he knew the Makololo didn't want them.

Thomas Baines, the artist who traveled with Livingstone and made drawings of his explorations

The disaster at Linyanti worried Livingstone even more because he was expecting another band of missionaries. Livingstone made it back to the mouth of the Zambezi to welcome them in January 1861. Bishop Mackenzie, their leader, was a man that even sour Charles Livingstone had to like. What's more, Livingstone's new steamer, the *Pioneer*, had arrived at the same time. The newcomers were soon sharing the life of the expedition, pulling the *Pioneer* over sand flats and suffering from malaria.

At Murchison Falls, they marched over to Magomero, a village Livingstone had selected for the mission. On the way, they began meeting slave caravans. The slavers ran from the missionaries, who enthusiastically began freeing the slaves, cutting their ropes and sawing through their taming sticks. By the time they got to Magomero, they had nearly one hundred fifty freed slaves with them. Shortly after their arrival, they set out to prevent an Ajawa raid on a nearby village. When Ajawa warriors began firing poisoned arrows, Livingstone gave the order to fire the guns. They killed six Ajawa and drove the rest off, but this committed the new missionaries to constant fighting. Livingstone was furious. He wrote, "People will not approve of men coming out to convert people by shooting them. I am sorry that I am mixed up with it."

The new missionaries arranged for their wives and their sisters to follow them. Livingstone went down to meet the women in the *Pioneer*, instructing Mackenzie to meet him at a point about halfway between the coast and Magomero. Because of sand flats, Livingstone was late in getting to the coast. The ship carrying the ladies had left to refuel. Mackenzie was afraid to miss the *Pioneer*, so he waited at the meeting point

Murchison Falls in Uganda

Livingstone's new steamboat, the Pioneer, *towing boats upstream*

on a barren island during the rainy season. On January 31, 1862, Livingstone was cheered to see the ladies' ship come into port. That same day, Mackenzie died of malaria, still waiting for Livingstone to return.

Livingstone's wife, Mary, was on the ship, too. Mary had come to stay with Livingstone in the Shire Highlands, but she wasn't the same woman she had been. In the past years, she had had to raise their five children alone, with little money and no real home. Now Livingstone feared she had lost her faith, as she constantly said bitter things about missionary work.

On the low, swampy coast, Mary got a bad case of malaria. Quinine didn't help. Livingstone was with her when she died on April 27. One man described Livingstone, "sitting by the side of a crude bed formed of boxes, but covered with a soft mattress, on which lay his dying wife. . . . The man who had faced so many deaths, and braved so many dangers, was now utterly broken down and weeping like a child."

In spite of his loss, Livingstone was determined to make it back up the Shire to Lake Nyasa. By now, the men on his expedition could hardly stand to work together, let alone unite for a trip as difficult as this would be. The year before, there had been very little rainfall. The people's crops had failed. Now there was famine all along the Shire. The men on the *Pioneer* saw bodies of people who had starved to death floating down the river. There was no food to be had.

Mary Livingstone's grave at an African mission station

Finally, John Kirk and Charles Livingstone asked to leave the expedition. Livingstone agreed. After six years of good service, he let Kirk go without even thanking him. Kirk was angry; he wrote,"He is about as ungrateful and slippery a mortal as I ever came in contact with . . . he is one of those sanguine enthusiasts wrapped up in their schemes whose reason and better judgment is blinded by headstrong passion."

With only a few American helpers, Livingstone started cutting down trees to build a road past the Murchison Falls, even though he knew he would not be able to finish even a small part of it before he ran out of supplies. In July 1863, he got word that his expedition had been recalled. At the same time, Livingstone had learned that the Magomero mission was to be withdrawn, too. By then, all but three of the missionaries had died.

Dr. Kirk of Edinburgh, Scotland, the naturalist who accompanied Dr. Livingstone in Africa

Livingstone returned to England. In the five years of the Zambezi expedition, he had added a great deal to European knowledge about the Zambezi and the Shire. Also, for the first time, he had given the British some idea of how extensive the East African slave trade was. But in his own eyes and the eyes of the public, he had failed to deliver anything he had promised. Instead of opening up Africa to European trade and Christianity, his expedition and the fate of the two missions had probably discouraged anyone from venturing there for many years to come.

Livingstone couldn't have known that, twenty years later, the Shire Highlands would become a British protectorate called Nyasaland, or that there would be a town on the Shire River named Blantyre, in honor of his own birthplace. In 1863, Livingstone knew he was going home a failure.

Chapter 6
In Search of the Nile

There were no celebrations, no banquets, when Livingstone came back to England in 1864. His wife's death in Africa made Livingstone realize, maybe for the first time, what a hard, lonely life she and his children had had. He hadn't seen any of his children for seven years, and he had never seen his youngest child, Anna Mary, who was born while he was setting off for the Zambezi. The little girl did not warm up to this stranger. He brought sweets for his oldest daughter, Agnes, only to realize that she was no longer a little girl but a woman of eighteen.

His oldest son, Robert, had an especially hard time adjusting to the narrow life in Britain after his free African childhood. Livingstone's letters to Robert had always been harsh and disapproving. Now Robert was fighting for the Union Army in the American Civil War. Robert changed his name in America because, as he wrote, "I am convinced to bear your name here would lead to further dishonors to it." Livingstone never saw his son again; Robert died in a Confederate prisoner-of-war camp in December 1864.

On this trip home, Livingstone asked friends, "Oh why did I not play more with my children in the Kolobeng days? Why was I so busy that I had so little time for my bairns [children]?" These regrets would not keep Livingstone in England; two years after this homecoming he was back on a ship, bound for Africa. The Royal Geographic Society had asked him to search for the source of the Nile River. Three other explorers had looked and come up with three different answers.

Livingstone still considered himself a missionary. Until the slave trade was abolished, Livingstone knew there was no hope for spreading the Christian faith in central Africa. The bad experience of the Magomero missionaries also showed it was futile for a handful of men to fight the slave trade alone. It would take government action to end it, and Livingstone would do what he could to spur his government to act. Exposing the slave trade, he decided, would be his missionary work.

For this trip, there was not much money, no steamer, no English assistants. Livingstone hired a small band of sixty-five porters to carry his trade goods and supplies. As an experiment, Livingstone brought along a group of animals—camels, buffalo, mules, and donkeys. He wanted to see if any of them would survive the bite of the tsetse fly. Once bitten by this insect, oxen, cows, and horses would slowly waste away and die. This is why every trading and exploring expedition had to hire porters to carry goods.

Livingstone put a group of men from India in charge of the animals. These men overloaded the animals, sometimes neglected to give them water, and beat them. Once they lagged behind to kill and eat one of the buffalo. When they told Livingstone a tiger had eaten it, he knew they were lying. There are tigers in India, but none in Africa. All the animals in the expedition died off, one by one, but Livingstone couldn't tell if it was from disease or mistreatment. He dismissed the Indians and went on with a smaller band of carriers.

On August 8, 1866, Livingstone reached Lake Nyasa. He had only eleven of his original band of sixty-five men. The Arab slave traders who sailed boats back and forth across the lake refused to carry Livingstone across. All of them had heard about Livingstone freeing the slaves in the Shire Highlands, and they didn't trust him. That meant Livingstone and his small band would have to walk around the lake. Then the rainy season began. Scrambling down a slippery slope, two porters fell. Livingstone's geographical instruments were damaged in the fall. From now on, all of his measurements would be twenty miles (thirty-two kilometers) off. Later, the man carrying Livingstone's medicines deserted, taking his load with him.

Now Livingstone had no defense against illness, but he couldn't face turning around and marching back 1,000 miles (1,609 kilometers). A few months later, Livingstone had a terrible attack of fever. He lay helpless in his tent for a month. His men hung a blanket across his doorway because they didn't want people to know how ill and weak their leader was. He couldn't have gone far even if he had been well. War had broken out between the Arab slave traders and the Africans in the area. With so few men and dwindling supplies, the only safe way for Livingstone to travel now was to march along with one of the Arab slave caravans.

These caravans were well armed and well supplied. If he traveled with them, Livingstone did not have to worry about buying food or paying tribute. Strangely enough, some of the Arab traders made a point of being kind and generous to him. Livingstone knew that these men were actually hunting for slaves. The caravans included long lines of men, women, and children in chains or on taming sticks. Nevertheless, Livingstone was able to tolerate traveling with them. He even became friendly with the Arab trader Mohammed Bogharib, who nursed him through several serious illnesses. If he wanted to pursue his work, Livingstone had to travel with the slave caravan.

He continued writing about the sad things he saw: "The strangest disease I have seen in this country seems really to be broken-heartedness, and it attacks free men who have been captured and made slaves. . . . One fine boy of about twelve years was carried, and when about to expire, was kindly laid down on the side of the path. . . . He, too, said he had nothing the matter with him except a pain in his heart . . . it seems to be really broken-hearts of which they die."

On the eighth of November, 1867, Livingstone reached Lake Mweru, a small lake on the border between present-day Zambia and Zaire. A river named the Luapula entered this lake at the south and the Lualaba flowed north out of the lake. Livingstone set two tasks for himself: one, to follow the Luapula south to find its source; the other, to follow the Lualaba north to see if it actually flowed into the Nile. Livingstone decided to head south for the source of the Luapula in the middle of the rainy season. This meant walking in waist-deep water for hours every day. In addition to the mosquitoes, the water was full of

A Lufembe slave hunter, engaged to help Arab slave traders

An exhausted captive, no longer of use to a vicious slave trader

leeches. Livingstone describes how hard it was to pull them off: "With fingers benumbed, though the water is only 60 degrees [16 degrees Celsius], one may twist them round the finger and tug, but they slip through. I saw the natives detaching them with a smart snap of the palm and found it quite effectual." They only covered about two miles (three kilometers) a day.

At the end of the rainy season, Livingstone finally reached Lake Bangweulu, the source of the Luapula River. His damaged instruments led him to miscalculate the size of the lake—he thought it was much bigger than it was. The rains also made the lake look much bigger because the land for miles around was actually a flooded swamp. These mistakes would hurt Livingstone later. For the moment, he felt confident that he had reached the source not only of the Luapula, but of the Lualaba and the Nile, too.

Livingstone rejoined Mohammed Bogharib; however, travel in the swamp had weakened him. When he was unable to walk, Bogharib had a litter, or stretcher, made for him. Livingstone was too weak to hold up a bunch of leaves to shade his face from the sun. Bogharib took him to Ujiji, where Livingstone expected to find supplies, medicines, and letters from home. He was disappointed to find only a fraction of the supplies he had ordered and no letters.

Livingstone next planned to go back to the Lualaba to see if it flowed into the Nile. However, he was stranded for eight months with ulcers—sores that refused to heal—on his feet. Livingstone had seen other men die from ulcers like these. The sores, he wrote, eat their way right through "muscle, tendon, and bone, and often lame permanently if they do not kill." Livingstone simply had to wait for the ulcers to heal. While he waited, he read through the Bible four times, becoming more and more dreamy and less and less scientific about his exploring task. He began hoping to find proof that the Hebrew leader Moses had traveled in central Africa. This gave his explorations a religious purpose and helped him to keep going.

After his feet healed, Livingstone marched to a market town called Nyangwe on the Lualaba in present-day Zaire. The Arabs here did not want to help Livingstone either. Although slavers had no trouble getting canoes, no one would sell or loan any to Livingstone, even though he offered all the money he had. On July 19, 1871, Livingstone witnessed an incident that made him "sick at heart." In the Nyangwe marketplace, three Arabs began to argue with an African over the price of a chicken. Suddenly the Arabs opened fire, shooting people at random. When the

David Livingstone at work on the journal of his explorations

crowd rushed for their canoes and tried to paddle out into the river, the Arabs followed. Livingstone wrote, "Shot after shot continued to be fired on the helpless and perishing. . . . One canoe took in as many as it could hold, and all paddled with hands and arms: three canoes, got out in haste, picked up sinking friends, till all went down together, and disappeared." Between 330 and 400 people were killed in Nyangwe.

Livingstone resolved that, no matter how needy he was, he could never allow himself to depend on slave traders again. He returned to Ujiji only to find that, once again, his supplies had been stolen. This was the point when Henry Stanley entered Livingstone's life. Livingstone had arrived in Ujiji on October 23, and Stanley arrived three weeks later.

Stanley would take Livingstone's description of the cold-blooded massacre at Nyangwe back to England. He couldn't talk Livingstone into going back to England with him, though. Livingstone did not want to return as a failure. He didn't realize that Stanley's description of him would turn him into an admired and beloved public figure, whether or not he had found the source of the Nile.

The two men treated one another with rare gratitude and respect. Stanley didn't see Livingstone's stubborn, vindictive side. The description he wrote of Livingstone seemed to erase the public's memory of the failed Zambezi expedition: "His gentleness never forsakes him; his hopefulness never deserts him. No harassing anxieties, distraction of mind, long separation from home and kindred, can make him complain. . . . Underneath that well-worn exterior lay an endless fund of high spirits and inexhaustible humor; that rugged frame of his enclosed a young and most exuberant soul. . . ."

While Stanley was raising Livingstone near to sainthood in people's eyes, Livingstone was traveling back into Africa to circle Lake Bangweulu and make sure it was the southernmost point of the Luapula. The mistaken measurements he had taken earlier now caused Livingstone to make a fatal mistake. Instead of following the advice of local inhabitants, he set his course by his old measurements and led his men into a swamp.

All the streams were swollen and had overflowed their banks, creating what Livingstone called sponges —grassy tufts floating on top of floodwater. Crossing streams meant wading through water that was sometimes waist-deep, sometimes chin-deep. By this time,

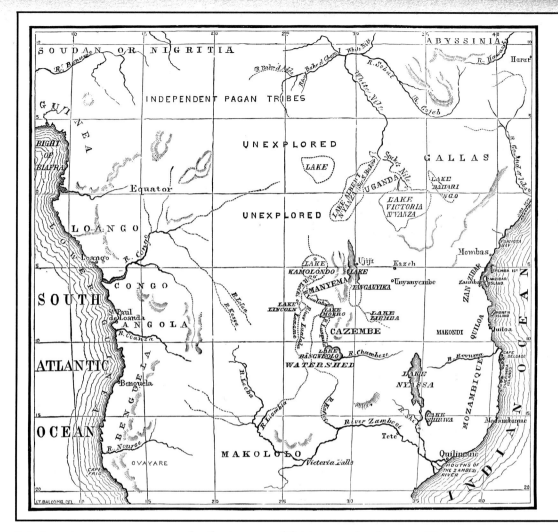

Livingstone was so weak that one of his men had to carry him across on his shoulders. On a good day they advanced a mile and a half (2.4 kilometers).

At night they looked for dry ground. One night, the high ground where they camped was the home of fierce red Siafu ants, also known as safari ants. Livingstone decided to test the idea that no animal will attack a human without being provoked. He waited while the ants swarmed over his foot and started biting. "I then went out of my tent and my whole person was instantly covered," he wrote. It took his men two hours to pick the ants off his body.

Nineteenth-century map of central Africa, showing many regions that Livingstone explored

Villages perched on dry islands in the lake. On one of these, Livingstone was able to get some canoes so his men could row through the bog instead of trudging through it. Travel in canoes was easier, but still very uncomfortable. Livingstone described canoeing for six hours to land on a bare island about ten yards (nine meters) across. There was no wood to make a fire, and the rain had drenched all their clothes and tents. They had to turn the canoes over for shelter from the rain, and sleep in wet, cold clothes.

Their tents had been soaked so many times that, on April 17, a hard rain ripped all of them to shreds. By now Livingstone had been suffering from diarrhea for so long that he was losing blood constantly. He recorded, "I am excessively weak. . . . I can scarcely hold the pencil, and my stick is a burden."

His men made a litter to carry him. Even the sway of the litter was very painful to Livingstone; he would be exhausted after being carried for an hour. On April 30, 1873, the expedition arrived at the village of a chief named Chitambo. Livingstone's men built him a hut there and helped him make some tea. One of the men slept right inside the door of the hut to tend to his needs in the night. At about four o'clock in the morning, the attendant woke to see that, in spite of his pain and weakness, David Livingstone had dragged himself off his low bed. He was kneeling against it, with his head in his hands, praying. He didn't move. David Livingstone was dead.

The men who had been with Livingstone the longest, Susi and Chuma, took charge. The easiest thing to do would have been to bury Livingstone there, but Susi decided to embalm Livingstone's body and take it to the coast, where an English ship could carry it

Livingstone's two loyal servants, Susi and Chuma

home. This was a tremendous feat of loyalty and endurance. Susi and Chuma held the sixty men together for the rest of the long trip back. Many tribes were superstitious about the dead. They demanded tribute to offset the bad luck of having a corpse carried through their territory. Livingstone's men had to fight their way out of one village. Finally, in February 1874, they arrived at Bagamoyo, a coastal city just across from the island of Zanzibar. A timid English official sent for a ship to collect the body. As the Africans' only reward for their suffering and bravery, the officer paid off their wages and sent them home.

Susi and Chuma spent almost a year carrying Livingstone's body back to the African coast.

Livingstone's body was shipped back to England. The lumpy bone of the left arm, where Livingstone had been bitten by the lion so many years ago, proved that it was indeed the body of the famous explorer. Livingstone was once again a national hero. Only those with tickets could get in to see his funeral service in London's Westminster Abbey. Crowds of people wept as the funeral procession passed by. One newspaper wrote: "Westminster Abbey had opened her doors to men who have played larger and greater parts in the history of mankind; but the feeling amongst many this afternoon was, that seldom has been admitted one more worthy—one more unselfish in his devotion to duty—one whose ruling desire was to benefit his kind and advance the sum of human knowledge and civilization—than the brave, modest, self-sacrificing, African explorer."

Leading the eight men who carried Livingstone's coffin into Westminster Abbey was Henry Stanley. When he learned of Livingstone's death in Africa, Stanley had written a letter to Livingstone's daughter: "How I envy you such a father. The richest inheritance a father can give his children is an honoured name. What man ever left a nobler name than Livingstone?"

Stanley himself had a great deal to do with raising the tremendous public admiration for Livingstone. He also suffered a great deal in doing it. Organizations like the Royal Geographic Society were hostile to this American interloper. Many said that Livingstone had rescued Stanley, and not the other way around. Some said that Stanley had forged some of Livingstone's maps and journals. Stanley finally won acceptance of his feat, but after Livingstone's death he saw another way to honor the man he admired and to prove himself once and for all to those who doubted him. He would carry on Livingstone's work. Livingstone had died before he could follow the Lualaba north. The source of the Nile River was still in question. In his journal Stanley wrote, "His mission, however, must not be allowed to cease; others must go forward to fill the gap. . . . May I be selected to succeed him in opening up Africa to the shining light of Christianity!"

David Livingstone's funeral in Westminster Abbey

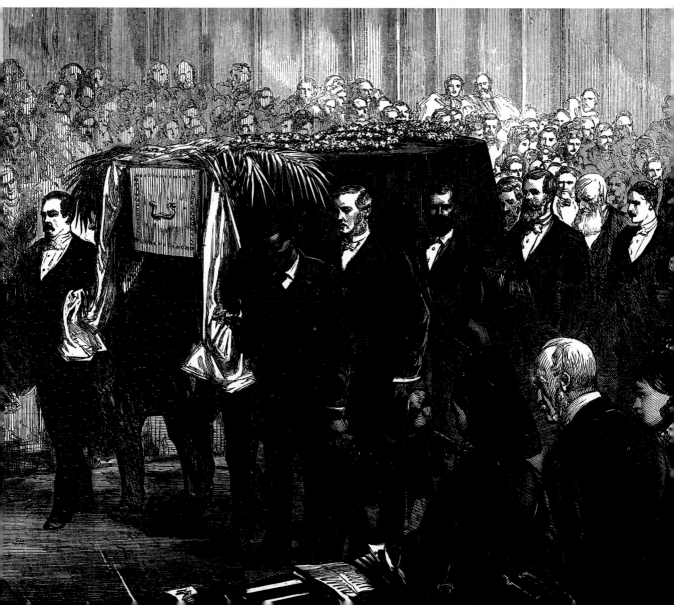

Chapter 7
The Decisive Crossing

Five months after David Livingstone's funeral, Stanley was back in Zanzibar hiring 356 porters and buying eight tons (7.2 metric tons) of supplies. He was about to embark on a trip that would take him 5,000 miles (8,047 kilometers) across Africa. He was funded this time by the *New York Herald* and a British newspaper, the *Daily Telegraph*. As usual, the terrible heat and hard work of hacking a path through the jungle immediately began to take its toll on the expedition. Stanley had counted on bartering for food, but there was a famine in the land they were crossing. There was nothing to eat but the rice they had brought.

Heavy rains soaked their camp; tents had to be pitched in the thick, cold mud. Frank Pocock, a man Stanley had brought from England as an assistant, wrote that they spent Christmas Day, 1874, drying their clothes. They managed to drive off an attack by local warriors, but twenty of their men were killed. Stanley pushed on; on February 27, 1875, they reached Lake Victoria. They had come through 720 miles (1,159 kilometers) of jungle and had only 166 of the original 356 people left.

The Lady Alice *in sections*

Frank Pocock

Lake Victoria was a huge expanse of water, dotted with islands. Explorer John Speke claimed that this lake was the source of the Nile. Stanley proposed to sail all the way around the lake, mapping it and noting all the rivers flowing into or out of it. For this purpose, he had had a special boat made. He named it the *Lady Alice*, after Alice Pike, the young fiancée he had left behind in New York. Henry and Alice had made a pact to remain faithful to one another until he returned, when they would be married. The boat had been carried to the lake in sections. Now Stanley had it put together and launched on the lake. For this trip, he took only a few men, leaving the rest in camp with Frank Pocock in charge.

Stanley knew he would be sailing past the kingdom of King Mutesa I, who ruled over the Baganda people. Mutesa's territory extended along the north-

King Mutesa I with some of his officers and chiefs

ern and western shores of Lake Victoria in what is now Uganda. As Stanley approached his shores, Mutesa sent six canoes to escort Stanley ashore. On landing, Stanley was met by two thousand Baganda, all dressed in robes of red, black, and white.

The king himself was a tall and imposing man. Mutesa was interested in widening his domain and resisting pressure from the Egyptian government to the north. He believed Stanley could help him. Stanley, for his part, wanted to describe Mutesa and his kingdom for the newspaper sponsors back in England and New York.

He also saw Mutesa and the Baganda as a people ripe for conversion to Christianity. Here Stanley seemed to be the true inheritor of Livingstone's mission. He talked to the king about Christianity and sent back a stirring call for missionaries.

Mutesa agreed to lend Stanley some warriors for the next leg of his journey. Meanwhile, Stanley set out to finish sailing around the west side of Lake Victoria. When it got to be time to make camp, Stanley and his men rowed to an island where the people seemed to beckon in a friendly way. When the boat drew close to shore, the people pulled it out of the water and surrounded Stanley and his crew. Some of the warriors grabbed the boat's oars, while others stood shaking their spears. Stanley sent a man named Safeni toward the chief with a gift and told the rest of the crew to push the boat back into the water as quickly as they could. The hostile warriors saw through this trick and came running at the boat. Stanley fired into the attackers and yelled at Safeni to dive into the water. With arrows falling all around them, the crew got the boat out to deeper water and tore some boards from the boat floor to use as oars. Safeni made it back to the *Lady Alice* and was pulled aboard.

Meanwhile, the island warriors chased them in four canoes. Stanley pulled out his elephant gun. His crew stopped rowing and let the canoes draw closer. Finally Stanley opened fire, and the powerful exploding balls sunk two of the canoes. The others turned back. Stanley and his men had escaped.

After Stanley returned to Mutesa's village, he vowed to take revenge on these island warriors. He sent a message threatening to attack unless they made amends. There was no answer. Stanley marshaled six canoes full of two hundred fifty men, some white and some Baganda. The canoes drew up to the island, and when the warriors came down to the water's edge, Stanley and his men began firing. This went on for an hour and a half. Stanley figured they had killed about

Mutesa's war canoes

thirty-three and wounded about a hundred. When he sent back a vivid description of this attack, readers in England and America were shocked. Stanley failed to realize the effect this dispatch would have.

Stanley had to wait another three months for the warrior escorts that Mutesa had promised. His plan was to march northwest to Lake Albert, another lake that had been claimed as the source of the Nile. The distance wasn't great, but they would be passing through the kingdom of the Banyoro people, the chief enemies of the Baganda. Finally, Stanley set out with his own men and more than two thousand Baganda. The way led first through waist-deep swamps. Bands of Banyoro warriors hid in the tall grass and shot volleys of arrows into Stanley's party. When they reached drier ground, they found that deep, hidden pits had been dug in their path.

By the time Stanley and his men came to a lake, there were thousands of warriors gathered around them. Stanley could see that, in the time it would take to put the *Lady Alice* together, they would all be killed. Moreover, both the Baganda and his own Zanzibari porters were terrified enough to desert the expedition rather than go into danger. Stanley led a hasty retreat back to Mutesa's kingdom. Even though Mutesa promised to send twenty-five thousand men along on his next attempt, Stanley would not risk going into Banyoro country again.

He turned south towards Ujiji and Lake Tanganyika. Nearly five years ago, Stanley had first greeted Livingstone in Ujiji. The town brought back memories of his dead friend. Livingstone and Stanley had sailed around part of Lake Tanganyika. This time, Stanley sailed all the way around the lake and proved that Lake Tanganyika had no connection with the Nile. Then he led his expedition west again, to Nyangwe on the Lualaba. Nyangwe was the market town where Livingstone had witnessed the terrible massacre of the Africans by Arab slave traders. Now the whole area was firmly under the control of one of the most powerful Arab traders in central Africa, Tippu Tip.

Tippu Tip

Tippu Tip controlled a vast area to the south and west of Lake Tanganyika. Either by force or by agreement, he had convinced the African chiefs in the area to sell their ivory and slaves only to him. In return, Tippu Tip offered protection from raids by other Africans or other traders and assured orderly markets and peaceful conditions. At their first meeting, Stanley was impressed by the intelligence and power of the Arab trader.

If Stanley followed the Lualaba north, he knew he

would be going into territory that had never been explored before. Not even the Arabs traded in this country because it was too dangerous. The people living there were very warlike. Rumors even circulated that they were cannibals, who ate their conquered enemies.

Terrified of going into this country, many of Stanley's men deserted. He needed reinforcements. Stanley offered to hire Tippu Tip and two hundred of his men to march along as protection. Stanley would pay him $5,000 for a sixty-day march. Tippu Tip agreed; besides, the Arab trader was interested in expanding his own territory. Exploring with Stanley would give him a chance to size up the area for trade.

On November 5, 1876, the expedition marched north into the jungle. Here the forest was so dense that it cut off most of the sunlight. Wet leaves dripped constantly on the men as they hacked a path through the gloomy jungle. In the villages they came across, there were rows of human skulls displayed on sticks. Stanley and one group launched the *Lady Alice* on the Lualaba and sailed down the river, while Tippu Tip led a group that marched down the banks. Stanley kept trying to barter for canoes, but the people along the river usually answered with poison arrows. As they marched, they could hear drums warning villages farther down the river of their approach. Tippu Tip was growing weary of this awful march. He told Stanley, "This country was not made for travel; it was made for vile pagans, monkeys, and wild beasts."

Tippu Tip decided to take his men back. Stanley feared that his followers would desert and go safely back with Tippu Tip, but the Arab leader said, "If any man follows me back to Nyangwe, I shall kill him."

The white-tailed colobus, a monkey native to Africa

Crossing the Lugungwa River

The trip did not get easier. Forty miles (sixty-four kilometers) of the river had waterfalls. The boats had to be taken out of the water and dragged along the riverbank. Stanley named this series of falls Stanley Falls (now called Boyoma Falls).

Once they got past the falls, the Lualaba spread out to as much as ten miles (sixteen kilometers) wide. The river no longer flowed north toward the Nile. Instead, it turned west and began to flow toward the

Atlantic Ocean. Livingstone had been wrong after all. The Lualaba River was the same stream as the westward-flowing Congo River.

Stanley shooting the rapids of the Congo River

The farther they sailed down the river, the more evidence of European influence they saw. Deep in the interior, none of the Africans had guns. Even when Stanley's men were outnumbered, their guns would win the day. But soon they found themselves being fired upon by warriors who loaded old Portuguese muskets with nails and pieces of metal. In all, the expedition fought thirty-two battles on the way down the river. The moments of peace were beautiful. Hippopotamuses would come up snorting, and many beautiful birds would fly along the river. But Stanley always had to be alert, scanning the shores and the islands to spot bands of war canoes.

Hippopotamus

On March 12, 1877, they were surprised to sail into a huge, calm, beautiful lake. Stanley named it after himself, calling it Stanley Pool (now Pool Malebo). Past the lake, they could hear the roaring sound of a waterfall. Once again, they would have to drag the boats along the riverbank. According to the local chief, there were three big falls ahead. Stanley was confident they could go around them. Out of a 7,000-mile (11,265-kilometer) trip, there were now only 150 miles (241 kilometers) between them and the west African coast. Had Stanley known the rapids and the falls would continue for miles, he might have decided to abandon the boats and simply march to the coast.

Stanley's men began muscling the boats over the slippery rocks on the riverbanks. Sometimes they used guide ropes to steer the boats from the shore, but the current was so strong that some of the boats were

Stanley traveling the Congo River

swept into the rock despite their efforts. The local Africans were not hostile, but they were not interested in Stanley's trade goods, either. Food was very scarce; the men began to faint from hunger. They had left Stanley Pool on March 1. By June 3, they had only covered 100 miles (161 kilometers), and the river was still a wild series of rapids and falls.

Finally, after three-and-a-half months of struggling to get around the rapids, Stanley saw that they would have to leave the boats and march overland to the nearest settlement, a place called Boma. Boma is about fifty miles (eighty kilometers) from the coast. He sent the three strongest men ahead with a letter begging for supplies: "I have arrived at this place from Zanzibar with 115 souls. . . . We are in a state of imminent starvation. We can buy nothing from the natives, for they laugh at our kinds of cloth, beads and wire. . . . What is wanted is immediate relief; and I pray you to use your utmost energies to forward it at once."

On August 7, 1877, relief arrived. Stanley's messengers returned leading porters with sacks of food. Two days later, they found an enthusiastic welcome in Boma. Stanley knew he had triumphed. Once again, the newspapers were eager to print every word he wrote about his journey. But this time, there were no accusations of forgery; Stanley was hailed everywhere as the greatest African explorer. In early 1878, he went back to England to a round of banquets and honors. His two-volume book *Through the Dark Continent*, which he wrote in just five months, was a wild success. Yet, after his African adventures, the easy life bored him, and he was brokenhearted, too. During his three-year trip across Africa, his fiancée, Alice Pike, had married someone else.

Chapter 8
Building the
Congo Free State

tanley was constantly urging the British government to step in and take a role in Africa's development. Like Livingstone, he believed that bringing Western trade to people along the Congo River would naturally bring Western civilization along with it. But no matter how much he wrote or talked about this scheme, the British weren't buying it. Merchants didn't see Africa as an important market; politicians didn't see it as England's mission to "civilize" central Africa. The only man who seemed to agree with Stanley about Africa was Leopold II, king of Belgium.

King Leopold had been looking for a colony. The newly explored Congo region looked like the opportunity he had been waiting for. Leopold hired Stanley to go back to the Congo for five years. His orders were to study the region's possibilities for development. To do this, Stanley would first have to build a road around the rapids near the river's mouth. Then he was to launch boats from Stanley Pool and begin building a series of stations or outposts along the river. Stanley had his own suspicions about this "study" and its purpose: "He [King Leopold] has not been so frank as to tell me outright what we are to strive for. Nevertheless it has been pretty evident that under the guise of an International Association he hopes to make a Belgian dependency of the Congo Basin."

Stanley left in 1879, sailing through the Mediterranean Sea and the Suez Canal, then down to Zanzibar to recruit porters. No one in Zanzibar knew what Stanley was up to this time, but he was able to recruit some of the men he and Livingstone had used before. With his men, Stanley sailed back up through the Mediterranean and down the west coast of Africa to the mouth of the Congo River. He arrived there on August 14, 1879.

On his earlier trip down to the Congo, Stanley had bartered for food with local people whenever he could. He fought with them when he couldn't avoid it. This trip would be very different. His instructions were to make treaties with all the chiefs along the river. He had to secure their goodwill, for they controlled traffic up and down the river.

The touchiest negotiations were with a chief named Ngalyema, who controlled the river just south of Stanley Pool. Ngalyema had a thousand fighters armed with muskets, so he could be a formidable enemy. Stanley opened by giving gifts—a Newfoundland dog, two monkeys, a mirror, a coat with gold embroidery, cloth—but Ngalyema was not satisfied.

Stanley expected trouble at their next meeting, so he placed some of his men in hiding and put a gong in front of his tent. When Ngalyema stormed out of the tent saying, "Enough! We do not want any white men among us," he noticed the gong and asked Stanley to strike it. Stanley protested, saying the gong would bring about war magic. Ngalyema insisted. When Stanley struck the gong, his men ran into the camp waving their weapons. Ngalyema's warriors ran in terror, and the chief himself hid behind Stanley. Gradually Ngalyema's men were coaxed back to camp.

Stanley's servant Sali, who worked for the explorer in Cairo, Egypt, and on his expeditions

Stanley with the African boy Kalulu and the interpreter Selim

They made peace over some palm wine, and Ngalyema consented to allow Stanley to build a settlement near Stanley Pool. The town Stanley founded—originally called Leopoldville—is now Kinshasa, the capital of Zaire.

Like Livingstone, Stanley enjoyed dealing with African chiefs. He, too, had developed a great appreciation for his Zanzibari men. Also like Livingstone, Stanley had very little patience in dealing with European assistants and administrators. Stanley reported to Colonel Maximillian Strauch, an army officer who supervised him from Belgium and had never been to Africa. Strauch was always trying to hurry Stanley along without any idea of the difficulties he faced.

Colonel Strauch

King Leopold II

After a year, Stanley had a near-fatal bout with malaria. He kept upping his dose of quinine—from twenty grains to fifty, then sixty—even though taking this much quinine was in itself dangerous. After fourteen days, Stanley was down to 100 pounds (45 kilograms). He was so weak he summoned his followers to give them his last orders and make his farewells. When his men arrived, he couldn't speak. Finally, he burst out, "I am saved." He fell unconscious, but his sense that he had passed out of danger was correct. In two weeks he was able to walk. As soon as he could, Stanley got back to work. In three years' time, he had built a road around the lower falls, launched two ships on the upper Congo, and set up five stations. This was more than he had promised to do in five years. Stanley decided to go home.

When he met Strauch in Belgium, to Stanley's shock, Strauch insisted that he go back and finish his five-year contract. King Leopold said, "Surely, Mr. Stanley, you cannot think of leaving me now, just when I most need you?" Leopold needed Stanley because the French had an explorer signing treaties with chiefs on the north side of Stanley Pool. Leopold was now personally paying 60,000 pounds (300,000 American dollars) a year to support Stanley's "study" of the Congo River Basin. He didn't want other countries edging in on his future colony.

Stanley went back. This time he was to make treaties with the African peoples upriver from Stanley Pool. As he steamed upriver, Stanley realized that, while opening the Congo for Europeans, he had also opened it to Arab slave traders. Once the Arabs saw that Stanley survived his trip down the Congo, they surged into this area where they had been afraid to

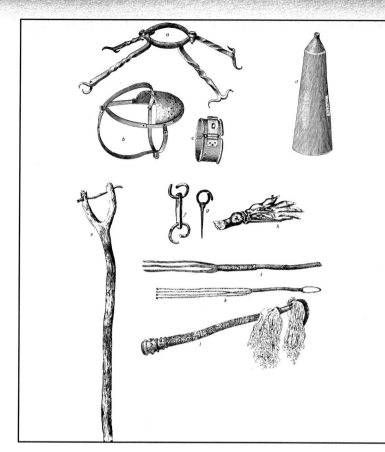

Instruments used in the slave trade to control captured people

venture before. In one Arab camp, Stanley saw more than two thousand natives, crowded in long huts, half-starved, and covered with sores from the constant rubbing of chains and slave collars.

In 1884, Stanley finished his five-year contract with Leopold. By this time, he had made four hundred treaties with chiefs and built stations all the way upriver to Stanley Falls. When Stanley got back to Europe, he found that Leopold's interest in the Congo had sparked other European nations to mark off their own territories in Africa. In November 1884, fourteen nations sent representatives to a meeting in Berlin, Germany, where they carved Africa into European colonies. The nations agreed to honor one another's claims to hundreds of thousands of square miles of African land.

Portrait of Henry Stanley

No African representatives were present. Their consent was not felt to be necessary. Of course, the colonizers expected that the new colonies would bring in wealth. The Africans would want to buy Western goods. Also, the Europeans could now use the natural resources of their African colonies. However, the Europeans also believed that they were taking over African territories for humanitarian reasons. Livingstone, Stanley, and other African explorers had written about the devastation of constant warfare and the horrors of the slave trade. Colonization, the Europeans believed, would end these two evils and bring peace and order to Africa.

King Leopold, through Stanley's efforts, claimed 900,000 square miles (2,331,000 square kilometers) around the Congo River. He named it the Congo Free State. Now that Stanley's hopes for the Congo Basin

An African ivory trader

were close to being fulfilled, Leopold kept him waiting on the sidelines. Stanley kept buying equipment for a return to the Congo, but his orders never came. Leopold no longer needed someone as colorful and fiery as Stanley. In fact, he wanted to keep Stanley quiet and out of the way.

When he made treaties with the chiefs along the river, Stanley told them he had come for "ivory and trade, and friendship." In the end, staying out of the Congo Free State was probably just as well for Stanley. His promise that men would come to buy ivory came true, but they did not come in friendship. Leopold used the Congo Free State for his own personal profit; his administrators ran the colony with a greed and cruelty that would be exposed by the British twenty years later. Eventually, Leopold was forced to hand the colony over to the Belgian government.

Chapter 9
Stanley to the Rescue

In December 1886, Stanley got the chance he had been yearning for—a chance to go back to Africa. He was asked to lead a rescue mission to a remote Egyptian province called Equatoria. In the 1870s, Egypt had extended its rule south through the Sudan as far as Equatoria. Part of present-day Uganda and southern Sudan, Equatoria stretched north from Lake Albert along the upper Nile River. When this territorial expansion put Egypt deeply in debt, the British took over managing the Egyptian budget in 1876 and occupied Egypt in 1882.

In 1881, under a Muslim religious leader called the Mahdi, the Sudanese rose up and pushed the British and Egyptians out of the Sudan. Nevertheless, Emin Pasha, the governor of Equatoria, continued to rule his territory for Egypt. The Mahdists had completely cut Equatoria off from Egypt; Emin Pasha wouldn't be able to hold out against them forever.

The British were stung by their defeat in the Sudan, and this kindled the fervor to rescue the loyal governor of Equatoria. A group of English businessmen put up 10,000 pounds (50,000 American dollars), believing that a rescue would also help spread English influence and trade. The British then decided that the Egyptian government should put up another 10,000 pounds. Everyone agreed that the only man to lead the rescue mission was Henry Morton Stanley.

Stanley eagerly consented. His plan was to recruit porters in Zanzibar, then sail south around the cape and up to the Congo River. He had Leopold's permission to use the Congo Free State's boats to sail 1,000 miles (1,609 kilometers) up the river. Then they would march 500 miles (805 kilometers) through the unexplored Ituri Forest to Equatoria.

In Zanzibar, Stanley was to pick up Leopold's newly appointed governor of the Stanley Falls area—none other than the Arab ivory and slave trader Tippu Tip. After Stanley built the Stanley Falls station, Arab traders had attacked it and driven the Belgians out. Now they had control of the upper Congo and were devastating the whole area.

Tippu Tip's contract gave him power "to defeat and capture all persons raiding the territory for slaves." Tippu Tip was well pleased to do this. He succeeded in making peace among the Belgians, the Arabs, and the Africans. As Stanley guessed, Tippu Tip used his authority to further his own ivory- and slave-trading empire. Appointing Tippu Tip did not end the slave trade; it only organized it along more peaceful and less brutal lines.

Stanley had met Tippu Tip during his first Congo trip, when the trader escorted him through some

An East African slaving raid in a village on market day

dangerous territory. The two had had trouble sharing command then, and Stanley was not looking forward to another difficult trip with the man. As before, however, Stanley knew he might need Tippu Tip's help in the interior. So he took Tippu Tip, his thirty-five wives, and about sixty servants on board for the trip around Africa to the Congo. Once the expedition disembarked and began to march up the river, their caravan stretched out for more than four miles (six kilometers). At Stanley Pool, they found an unpleasant surprise. The boats that were to transport them up to Stanley Falls were in ruins. In desperation, Stanley simply took over every boat he could find, no matter whose it was. One missionary wrote that he felt he had better graciously lend Stanley his boat: "Had we not done so with good grace he would have taken her by force. This is no suspicion—we know it."

At Stanley Falls, Stanley split up his men; he left a young English officer named Edward Barttelot in charge of a camp there. Barttelot was to supervise bringing their supplies upriver, gather six hundred porters promised by Tippu Tip, and then march into the forest after Stanley. Meanwhile, Stanley led 389 men into the forest to relieve Emin Pasha as soon as possible. Stanley expected to be back to the camp in four months' time; he thought it was at the most about 550 miles (885 kilometers) to Equatoria.

The distance was actually 700 miles (1,127 kilometers) through a dense, hot, and gloomy forest. The march began at six every morning and ended at about four, when everyone had to work on building huts for the night. Stanley described what nighttime in the camp was like: "By nine o'clock the men, overcome by fatigue, would be asleep; silence ensued, broken only by sputtering fire-logs, flights of night-jars, hoarse notes from great bats, croaking of frogs, cricket-cheeps, falling of trees or branches, a shriek from some prowling chimpanzee, a howl from a peevish monkey, and the continual gasping cry of the lemur. But during many nights, we would sit shivering under ceaseless torrents of rain, watching the forky flames of the lightning, and listening to the stunning and repeated roars of the thunder-cannonade, as it rolled through the woody vaults."

After a month of travel in the dim light and thick undergrowth of the forest, Stanley's men began to lose heart. They were low on food. Stanley shot his own riding donkey to feed his men and watched them fight over pieces of the meat. He had to send men out into the forest to forage for anything edible; they came back with berries and locusts.

Major Edward M. Barttelot, one of Stanley's assistants

African pygmy family

With the men weakened by hunger, even small cuts began turning into terrible ulcers. Some men died of illness; some went mad and ran off into the forest. Some were killed by the poison arrows of the pygmies, short people who lived deep in the jungle. A shot of ammonium would counteract the poison, but it had to be done quickly, before the victim died. In the last seventy days of the forest trek, 180 of Stanley's men either died or deserted. After 162 days, the expedition finally came out of the forest into an open grassland. Stanley wrote that the open sky and countryside looked to him like a "grassy Eden." In the first moments of exhilaration, Stanley and his men broke into a joyous run. A week later, the expedition reached Lake Albert.

In March 1888, the rescuers finally met Emin Pasha. He came cruising across Lake Albert in his steamship. By the light of bonfires, Emin and Stanley shook hands while Stanley's men fired jubilantly into the air. Then the men sat down on boxes to share the champagne that Stanley had brought. As they looked each other over, Emin looked more like the rescuer than Stanley. While Stanley and his men were thin and their clothes were in tatters, Emin was smartly dressed and well provided with food.

Although he was grateful for the thirty-one cases of ammunition that Stanley had brought, Emin was reluctant to be "rescued." Actually a German, Emin was born Eduard Carl Schnitzer. He had served as a medical officer in Turkey, where he adopted Turkish

Ceremony conferring the title of Pasha on Emin

dress and changed his name. In 1878, he was appointed governor of Equatoria. Emin was a cultured man who played the piano very well. Also an avid naturalist, he had assembled a huge collection of stuffed African birds, which he meant to give to the British Museum. At first, Emin seemed to have no intention of leaving with Stanley.

Emin Pasha

Stanley did not want to return to Zanzibar without Emin Pasha after losing so many lives and spending so much money. He went back through the forest to collect the men he had left in camp near Stanley Falls. Barttelot had never come up with the supplies, even though the path had been carefully marked.

Stanley had told Barttelot that he would be back by November 1887. He actually returned on August 19, 1888. While he was gone, things had fallen apart. Barttelot was dead, as were 210 of the 270 men from camp. The surviving Zanzibaris were so weak with hunger that they could no longer walk; they crawled to greet their returning companions. The one remaining Englishman told Stanley what had happened.

In the first place, Tippu Tip delayed in sending the porters he had promised. Finally he sent four hundred instead of six hundred, and insisted that they each carry loads of forty rather than sixty pounds (eighteen rather than twenty-seven kilograms).

When the porters arrived and Barttelot finally started through the Ituri Forest, the march was slow and undisciplined. Tippu Tip had told his men that if Barttelot treated them badly, they should shoot him. One morning in July 1888, Barttelot was annoyed by an African woman drumming loudly in the camp. When he began to argue with her, her husband, a chief, shot Barttelot through the heart.

Stanley knew he had left Barttelot with a difficult job. Nevertheless, Stanley put the blame for this disaster squarely on Barttelot's shoulders. He refused to admit he had been even partially responsible. On his last trip to Africa, Stanley was desperate to succeed.

Now he took the weak survivors back through the forest one last time to combine all his forces in Equatoria. While Stanley was gone, the Mahdists had raided Equatoria. The raid showed how weak Emin's following really was. Many of his soldiers deserted to the other side and launched a rebellion.

Equatoria was in chaos. Stanley announced that he was leaving on April 10, 1889. He would take along Emin and any of his followers who made it to camp by that time. About six hundred men, women, and children joined the march. Some brought almost nothing. Others were weighed down with bed frames, tin bathtubs, and other possessions. Stanley raided the countryside to find five hundred local Africans to serve as porters. Then the unwieldy caravan of about fifteen hundred people started the long walk to Zanzibar. Of the six hundred refugees from Equatoria, only 246 lived through the trip.

Stanley had rescued Emin Pasha. He had neither made Equatoria part of the Congo Free State, as Leopold wished, nor joined it to Uganda, as the British merchants wished. Equatoria had sunk into anarchy; it had no organized government any more. The ammunition Stanley had taken to Emin was either stolen by rebels or buried to keep it out of Mahdist hands. The rescue expedition had suffered terrible loss of life—about two hundred of Stanley's original seven hundred men survived. Yet when Stanley reached the coast, he found himself hailed as a hero.

Stanley rescuing Emin Pasha

On Stanley's and Emin's first evening back on the East African coast, the German embassy hosted an elaborate banquet in their honor. The banquet was held in a second-floor dining hall. After dinner, wine, and speeches, Emin stepped out onto a balcony to smoke a cigar. A few moments later there was an outcry in the street. Stanley rushed down to find that Emin had fallen over the balcony and lay in the street. After months of dangerous travel, Emin Pasha had nearly lost his life at a dinner party.

Emin survived, but he made a decision that disappointed his British rescuers. He decided to stay in East Africa and work for the Germans in what is now Tanzania. This meant that Emin would be heading right back into the regions from which he had just been rescued. A few years later, he was killed near Stanley Falls, beheaded by an Arab slave trader.

Chapter 10
Bula Matari Goes Home

Whether or not Emin had been worth rescuing, Stanley was acclaimed all over Europe and America for rescuing him. He received piles of congratulatory telegrams, including messages from U.S. president Benjamin Harrison, Great Britain's Queen Victoria, the khedive of Egypt, and King Leopold of Belgium. By this time, there were also songs, poems, and plays about him. In England people were even selling mugs with his picture on them. When he returned to England in May 1890, welcoming crowds thronged to see him wherever he went. *In Darkest Africa*, his account of Emin's rescue, became a best-seller in several languages.

Among the many invitations Stanley received was one from an artist named Dorothy Tennant. Stanley had fallen in love with her four years earlier, before he went on the Emin rescue mission. He had asked her to marry him then, and she had refused. Now she wrote apologizing for rejecting him and begging him to reconsider. Stanley was persuaded.

On July 12, 1890, he and Dorothy Tennant were married in Westminster Abbey. The church was packed with those prominent or powerful enough to win invitations—politicians, explorers, nobility. Five thousand requests for invitations had to be turned down. The bride wore wedding jewels given to her by Queen Victoria, King Leopold, and Stanley himself. Instead of throwing her bouquet, Dorothy Stanley lay it on the tomb of David Livingstone.

Stanley's groomsmen were the five English officers who had survived the Emin expedition. Sadly, only two of these five men would be alive three years later; the expedition had ruined their health. Stanley himself would have recurring attacks of gastritis (severe stomach pain) and malaria for the rest of his life. He had one such attack on his wedding day.

During the service, he had to sit in an armchair; afterwards, he was barely able to escort the bride down the aisle. During their honeymoon in the country, Stanley recovered. But Dorothy Stanley wrote about how much they dreaded the recurring malaria attacks, which began with uncontrollable shivering "so violent that the bed he lay on would shake, and the glasses on the table vibrate and ring."

When he was feeling well, Stanley was in great demand as a speaker. William MacKinnon, the merchant who had organized the funding for the Emin Pasha expedition, wanted to hire Stanley to go back to Africa and oversee the ventures of MacKinnon's Imperial British East Africa Company. But Dorothy didn't want him to go back. She wrote, "I knew that he ought never to return there."

Dorothy urged Stanley to run for the Parliament, Great Britain's lawmaking body. In 1895, he was

Henry Stanley on his return from Africa

Dorothy Tennant Stanley

elected to the House of Commons for a five-year term. Stanley did not enjoy his position in Parliament, though; he found it frustrating and confining. He wasn't interested in most of the issues discussed. Africa had changed so quickly during the time he had been away that he was no longer an expert, even on African policy. Africa was now divided up into colonies run by administrators. The work of exploration was done.

In 1899, the Stanleys moved to a house they called Furze Hill, thirty miles (forty-eight kilometers) from London. They named the creek on their property the Congo, and they called their little lake Stanley Pool. In January 1901, Stanley turned sixty years old. His fame as an explorer had faded. His achievements were overshadowed by reports of the viciousness of Leopold's regime in the Congo Free State.

In April 1903, he was partly paralyzed by a stroke. In May 1904, Dorothy Stanley could see that her husband was dying. On the morning of his death, Stanley looked at his wife and said, "I want—I want—to go home." He died at about six o'clock in the morning on May 10, 1904. One of Stanley's last wishes had been to be buried in Westminster Abbey beside Livingstone, but the dean of the abbey refused. After a service in Westminster, Stanley was buried in the village churchyard near Furze Hill.

Stanley may have been the greatest of all the African explorers. His persistence and determination to succeed carried him through feats that no other African explorer could equal. After his death, a writer surveyed Stanley's accomplishments: "The map of Africa is a monument to Stanley. . . . It was Stanley who gathered up the threads, brought together the loose ends, and united the discoveries of his predecessors into one coherent and connected whole.

Stanley's work led directly to the European nations' "scramble for Africa." By the time he died, steamship lines and railroads were gradually making the long lines of porters unnecessary. The slave trade that he and Livingstone had hated had come to an end. Most of Africa had been claimed and was now administered by European powers. Stanley's single-handed efforts had had a tremendous effect on Africa's political future. Still, Europeans did not bring to Africa all the "blessings" of Christianity that Livingstone and Stanley had envisioned. Although missionaries did come, colonization also meant exploitation and the destruction of African ways of life.

Stanley had always admired Livingstone's unselfishness and gentleness. Stanley himself was not a

Stanley writing his book

gentle man. Accomplishing what he did took relentless willpower. He had to push both himself and his followers through awful dangers and difficulties. Many of them died or ruined their health in the process. No obstacle seemed enough to stop him. Because of his road-building fervor, the Africans he worked with in the Congo had a special name for Stanley—Bula Matari, "the Smasher of Rocks."

Yet Stanley's goals for Africa had been largely shaped by Livingstone. Stanley never bought any shares in any of the African enterprises he inspired. Once when he was accused of pushing African colonization to further his own financial interests, Stanley agreed that he had an interest in Africa, but not a profit-making one: "My whole interest there is for Africa herself, and for humanity."

Appendix

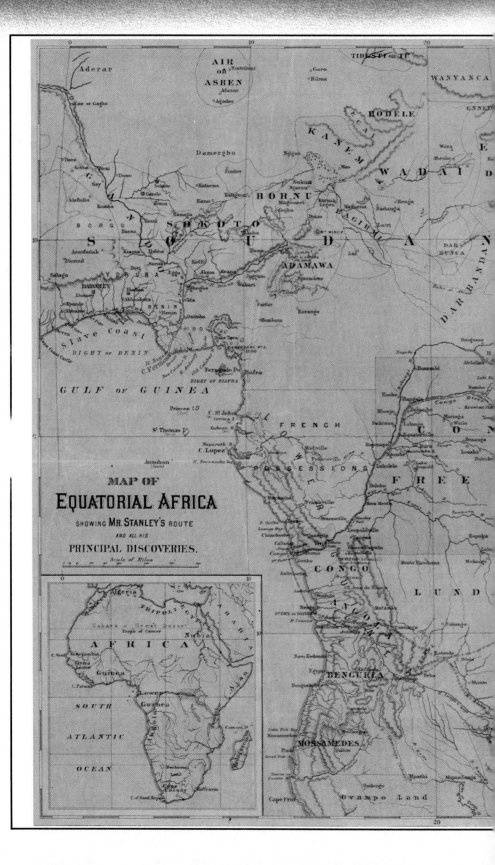

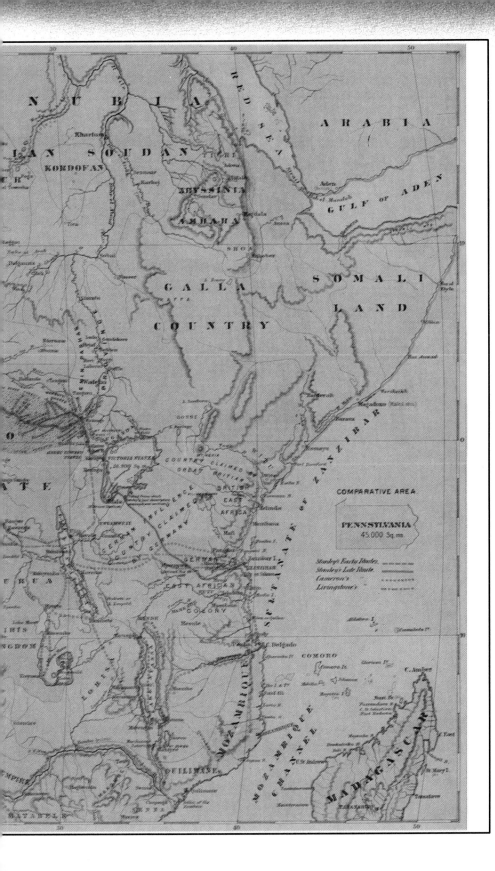

119

Timeline of Events in Stanley's and Livingstone's Lifetimes

1813—David Livingstone is born on March 19 in Blantyre, Scotland

1823—At the age of ten, Livingstone goes to work in a textile mill

1836—Livingstone enters Anderson College in Glasgow, Scotland

1840—Livingstone receives his medical certificate from Glasgow University and is sent to Africa by the London Missionary Society

1841—Henry Morton Stanley [John Rowlands] is born on January 28 in Denbigh, Wales; Livingstone arrives in southern Africa and begins his ministry in Kuruman

1843—Livingstone moves north and settles in Mabotsa

1845—Livingstone marries Mary Moffat

1849—With two companions, Livingstone is the first European to cross the Kalahari Desert and see Lake Ngami

1851—Livingstone discovers the Zambezi River and Victoria Falls

1854—Livingstone reaches the Atlantic Ocean at Luanda in present-day Angola

1856—Livingstone reaches Quelimane on the East African coast, becoming the first European to cross Africa from coast to coast

1858—Stanley signs on as a cabin boy on a ship sailing to New Orleans; Livingstone leaves England for an expedition up the Zambezi River

1862—Mary Moffat Livingstone dies; as a Confederate soldier in the American Civil War, Stanley fights at the Battle of Shiloh; he is taken prisoner by Union forces and sent to a prisoner-of-war camp in Chicago, where he changes to the Union side

1864—After the Zambezi expedition, Livingstone returns to England

1866—Livingstone returns to Africa to find the source of the Nile

1867—Stanley becomes a reporter for the *St. Louis Democrat* and then for the *New York Herald*, whose editor sends him to Abyssinia

1869—Stanley is assigned to find Livingstone

1871—Stanley finds Livingstone at Ujiji

1873—David Livingstone dies on May 1 while exploring the Lualaba River basin

1874—Livingstone's body is buried in Westminster Abbey; Stanley embarks on his expedition to establish the source of the Nile

1878—On his return to England, Stanley writes *Through the Dark Continent*, an account of his travels through Africa

1879—Commissioned by Leopold II of Belgium, Stanley returns to the Congo Basin for five years to establish stations along the river

1887—Stanley leads an expedition to rescue Emin Pasha, governor of Equatoria

1890—Stanley returns to England, publishes *In Darkest Africa*, and marries Dorothy Tennant

1892—While leading a German expedition into central Africa, Emin Pasha is murdered

1895—Stanley takes a seat in Parliament

1899—Stanley is knighted

1904—Henry Morton Stanley dies on May 10 at Furze Hill, his home near London

Glossary of Terms

alcove—A small room or section of a room

anarchy—The absence of a ruler or of law and order

baptism—A ceremony of initiation into Christianity

caravan—A long procession of travelers

converts—People who have accepted and joined a certain religion

daunted—Subdued; frightened; unnerved

dormitory—A large room or building where people can sleep

drought—A period of hot, dry weather that makes crops wither

dysentery—An infectious disease causing severe stomach pains and diarrhea

electrify—To excite or charge with energy

famine—A period of crop failure and food shortage

fiasco—A total failure

forge—To make a false or misleading document

germs—Microscopic organisms that cause diseases

gruel—A soup made of boiled beans or grains

hearsay—Information based on rumors instead of on hard facts

indefatigable—Never tiring

interloper—Someone who interferes with another person's rights

irrigation—The bringing of water to farmland, usually by digging ditches from a river or lake

khedive—A ruler of Egypt governing as a representative of the Turkish sultan

litter—A covered couch carried on poles or a stretcher for carrying a sick person

malaria—A disease caused by parasites that are carried by mosquitoes

marauding—Raiding in order to rob

mildew—A fungus that grows on the surface of materials under moist conditions

mirage—An optical illusion in which water appears over the surface of the desert, a pavement, or some other hot surface

mission—A religious ministry to spread a faith

missionary—A person on a religious mission

pamphlet—A small printed publication made entirely of paper or having a soft cover

porter—A person who carries baggage

pound—A British unit of money; in the late 1800s, one pound was equal to about five American dollars

roving—Moving from place to place

sensational—Arousing great interest or curiosity

staunch—Strong in loyalty or beliefs

sultan—A ruler in an Islamic country

tropical—Occurring in the hot regions just north and south of the equator

vagrant—A homeless person, usually having no money, who wanders from place to place

Bibliography

For further reading, see:

Farrant, Leda. *Tippu Tip and the East African Slave Trade.* London: Hamish Hamilton, 1975.

Hall, Richard. *Stanley: an Adventurer Explored.* London: Collins, 1974.

Huxley, Elspeth J. *Livingstone and His African Journeys.* New York: Saturday Review Press, 1974.

Jeal, Tim. *Livingstone.* London: Heinemann, 1973.

Livingstone, David. *The Last Journals of David Livingstone in Central Africa.* 2 vols. Westport, CN: Greenwood, 1968. Reprint of 1874 edition.

———. *Missionary Travels and Researches in South Africa.* Salem, NH: Arno, 1972. Reprint of 1857 edition.

McEvedy, Colin. *The Penguin Atlas of African History.* Harmondsworth, England: Penguin, 1980.

Simmons, Jack. *Livingstone and Africa.* London: English Universities Press, 1955.

Stanley, Henry Morton. *The Autobiography of Sir Henry Morton Stanley.* Dorothy Stanley, ed. Boston: Houghton Mifflin, 1909.

———. *How I Found Livingstone: Travels, Adventures, and Discoveries in Central Africa.* New York: Negro Universities Press, 1969. Reprint from New York: Scribner's, 1913.

Ungar, Sanford. *Africa: the People and Politics of an Emerging Continent.* New York: Simon & Schuster, 1986.

Index

Page numbers in boldface type indicate illustrations.

Picture Identifications for Chapter Opening Spreads

6–7—Rising sun over the Chobe River in Chobe National Park, Botswana

20–21—City scene of Glasgow, Scotland

28–29—New Orleans, Louisiana

38–39—Victoria Falls, Zimbabwe

56–57—Shire River and valley in southern Malawi

68–69—Cattle egrets in Ndutu, Tanzania

82–83—White pelicans in Tanzania

94–95—Flamingoes gathered offshore

102–103—The Zambezi River, Zimbabwe

112–113—The jacana, or lilytrotter, of Africa

Picture Acknowledgments

THE BETTMANN ARCHIVE: 62

HISTORICAL PICTURES SERVICE, CHICAGO: 2 (2 photos), 5, 8, 14, 15, 20–21, 22, 24, 28–29, 34, 35, 36, 41, 43, 47, 52, 58, 61, 63, 67, 75, 77, 79, 81, 84 (top), 91 (top), 97, 98 (2 photos), 105, 111, 114, 115

© EMILIE LEPTHIEN: 54

NORTH WIND PICTURE ARCHIVES: 9, 10, 11, 33, 45, 55, 65, 66, 72, 73, 78, 84 (bottom), 85, 87, 96, 99, 101, 106, 108, 109, 117

PHOTRI: 4, 6–7, 13, 37, 56-57, 64, 92, 100

TOM STACK & ASSOCIATES: © THOMAS KITCHIN, 91 (bottom)

SUPERSTOCK INTERNATIONAL, INC.: © RUDY GRUBERG, 107

VALAN: © AUBREY LANG, 38–39, 102–103; © STEPHEN J. KRASE-MANN, 68–69, 82–83, 94–95; © J.A. WILKINSON, 112–113

© VISION QUEST: 49, 88, 89, 90, 118–119

COVER ILLUSTRATION BY STEVEN GASTON DOBSON

About the Author

Susan Maloney Clinton holds a Ph.D. in English and is a part-time teacher of English Literature at Northwestern University in Chicago. Her articles have appeared in such publications as *Consumer's Digest, Family Style Magazine,* and the Chicago *Reader*. In addition, she has contributed biographical and historical articles to *Encyclopaedia Britannica* and *Compton's Encyclopedia*, and has written reader stories and other materials for a number of educational publishers. Ms. Clinton lives in Chicago with her husband, Pat, and their children.